FIRST 50 LICKS
YOU SHOULD PLAY ON GUITAR

by Troy Nelson

ISBN 978-1-5400-3062-7

Visit Hal Leonard Online at
www.halleonard.com

Contact us:
Hal Leonard
7777 West Bluemound Road
Milwaukee, WI 53213
Email: info@halleonard.com

In Europe, contact:
Hal Leonard Europe Limited
42 Wigmore Street
Marylebone, London, W1U 2RN
Email: info@halleonardeurope.com

In Australia, contact:
Hal Leonard Australia Pty. Ltd.
4 Lentara Court
Cheltenham, Victoria, 3192 Australia
Email: info@halleonard.com.au

CONTENTS

LICK 1
Back to the (ZZ) Top

MUSICAL STYLE: Blues Rock

SOUNDS LIKE: Billy Gibbons

OVERVIEW: This lick sounds a lot like a Delta blues turnaround, but instead of moving from the I chord to the V chord at the midpoint of bar 2, this lick sticks with the I chord (in this case, A) throughout. Listen to ZZ Top's "La Grange" for a lick similar to the one shown here.

TIP: Keep your pinky planted on fret 5 of string 1 while you walk down string 4 with your ring, middle, and index fingers, respectively.

 Key of A

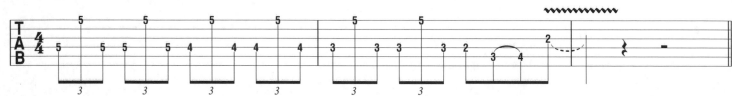

 **Key of C**

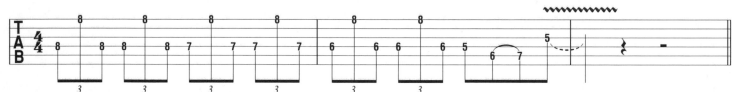

 **Key of D**

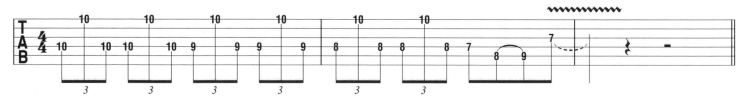

 **Key of G**

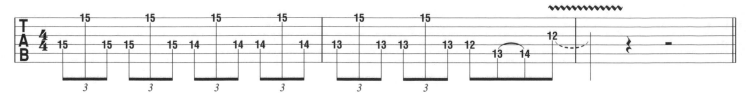

LICK 2
Beck Bends

MUSICAL STYLE: Blues Rock

SOUNDS LIKE: Jeff Beck

OVERVIEW: Whereas most guitarists favor whole-step unison bends, Jeff Beck has an affinity for the half-step variety, often incorporating open strings as in the lick shown here. The notes are derived from the Mixolydian pentatonic scale (1–3–4–5–♭7), which differs from the ubiquitous minor pentatonic scale (1–♭3–4–5–♭7) by just one note (the former contains a major 3rd; the latter a minor 3rd).

TIP: Fourth-string bends, especially near the nut, can be challenging, so use your middle or ring finger for the bend, reinforcing it with your other fingers. For the third-string bends in the subsequent licks, use your pinky to bend, backing it up with your ring and middle fingers.

Key of A

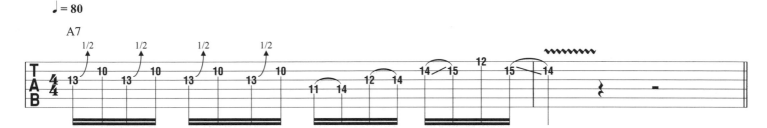

Key of D

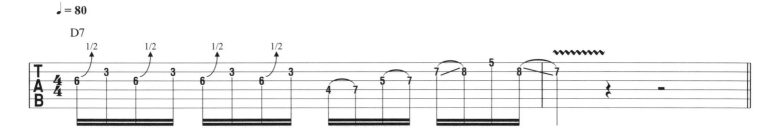

Key of E

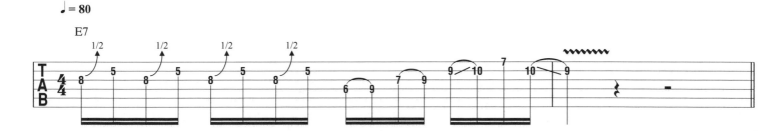

Key of G

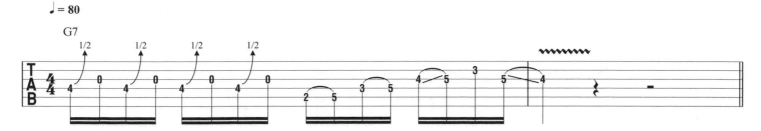

LICK 3
Been Caught Steelin'

MUSICAL STYLE: Country

SOUNDS LIKE: James Burton

OVERVIEW: Nothin' says "country guitar" quite like steel-guitar licks. Most of the notes in this phrase are rooted in the ninth-position E major pentatonic box (E–F#–G#–B–C#), with a couple of notes from E Mixolydian (D note on fret 12, string 4) and E minor pentatonic (G note on fret 10, string 5) thrown in for good measure.

TIP: Bend with your ring finger (reinforced with your middle) and, while holding the bend, use your index and pinky fingers for the notes on strings 1 and 2, respectively. (For the G lick, bend with your middle finger, using your pinky for the note on string 2.)

 Key of E

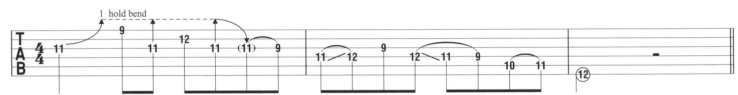

 Key of G

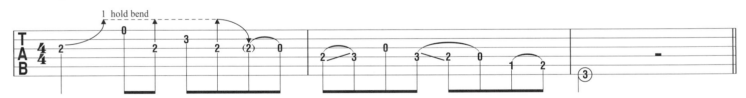

 Key of C

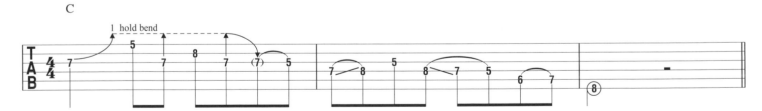

 **Key of D**

LICK 4
Bend It Like B.B.

MUSICAL STYLE: Blues

SOUNDS LIKE: B.B. King

OVERVIEW: If you're familiar with the five patterns ("boxes") of the minor and/or major pentatonic scale, then you'll notice this lick is rooted in pattern 3, also known as the "B.B. King box" due to its namesake's propensity to play licks in this location. The phrase draws its notes from both the minor and the major versions of the scale and features well-placed half- and whole-step bends.

TIP: Slide into the lick with your middle finger, voicing the notes at frets 9 and 10 with your index finger.

 Key of A

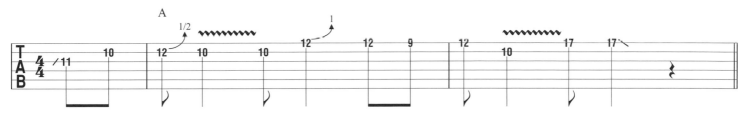

 Key of B

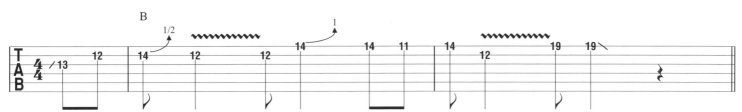

 Key of E

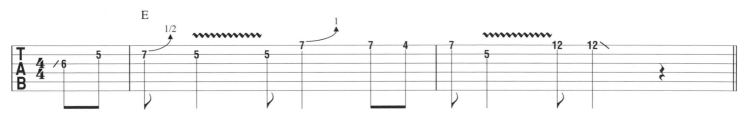

 Key of G

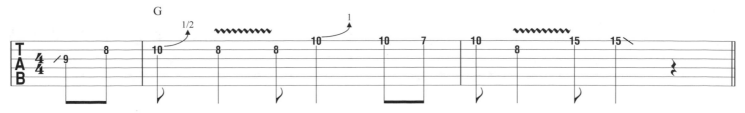

LICK 5
Berry Goode Bends

MUSICAL STYLE: Early Rock 'n' Roll

SOUNDS LIKE: Chuck Berry

OVERVIEW: No lick gets more action from guitar players than this one! You can hear it in everything from early blues and rock 'n' roll to modern-day hard rock and metal. Chuck Berry made it famous, but historians often cite Texas bluesman T-Bone Walker for its creation.

TIP: Use a two-string index-finger barre for the fifth-fret notes and execute the bend with your ring finger, reinforced with your middle.

 Key of A

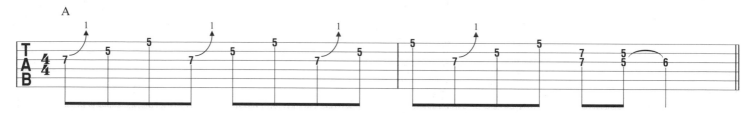

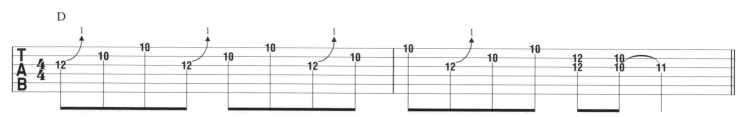 **Key of D**

 Key of E

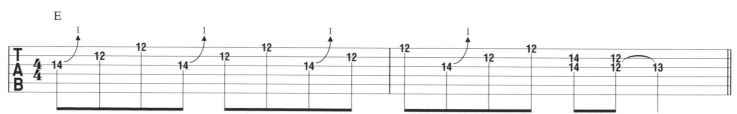

Key of G

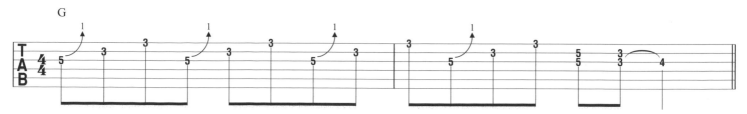

LICK 6
Buddy's Blues

MUSICAL STYLE: Blues

SOUNDS LIKE: Buddy Guy

OVERVIEW: This phrase is a great example of the previous Chuck Berry lick being used in a different context—in this case, the blues. After the initial "Berry bend," half- and whole-step bends, hammer-ons, pull-offs, and vibrato are used to squeeze a whole lot of emotion into this short, two-bar phrase, which is firmly planted in the D blues scale (D–F–G–G♯–A–C).

TIP: For maximum "bluesiness," be sure to limit the second 12th-fret bend to a half step.

Key of D

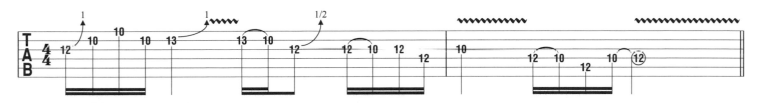

Key of E

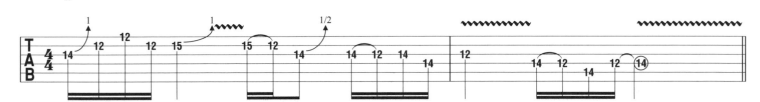

Key of G

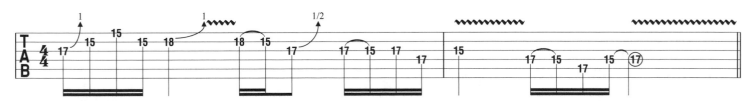

Key of A

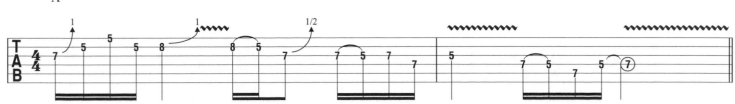

LICK 7
Built for Speed

MUSICAL STYLE: *Rockabilly*

SOUNDS LIKE: Brian Setzer

OVERVIEW: This lick is straight out of the Brian Setzer playbook. You'll hear similar versions of this phrase on early Stray Cats recordings and, later, on his swing albums with the Brian Setzer Orchestra. The pitches are derived from the A Dorian mode (A–B–C–D–E–F#–G) and are executed via three-note pull-offs played in an eighth-note-triplet rhythm.

TIP: Be sure to swing the eighth notes that punctuate the pull-offs, playing the upbeats slightly shorter than the downbeats.

 Key of A

 Key of D

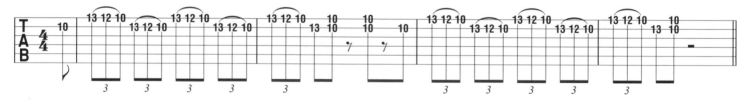

Key of E

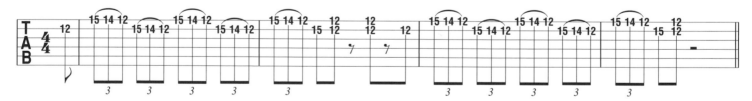

Key of G

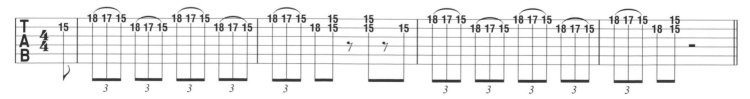

LICK 8
Cannonball Run

MUSICAL STYLE: Blues

SOUNDS LIKE: Freddie King

OVERVIEW: Nicknamed the "Texas Cannonball," Freddie King was known for his blistering hammer-ons, and this lick is a good example of his style. A turnaround phrase, the lick represents the last three bars of a 12-bar blues, starting with the IV (A) chord before moving to the I (E) chord and culminating with the V (B) chord.

TIP: Be sure not to rush the triplets in measure 1. All three notes of each beat have equal rhythmic value, so make sure you perform the hammer-ons in time.

 Key of E

 Key of G

 Key of A

 Key of D

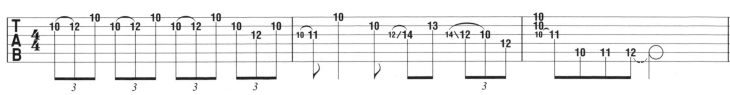

LICK 9
Country Boy Twang

MUSICAL STYLE: Country

SOUNDS LIKE: Albert Lee

OVERVIEW: This lick is a crash course in country double stops, or "dyads." It starts with a hammer-on figure in ninth position (measure 1) before shifting to 12th position for some more double-stop action. At the midpoint of measure 2, the phrase uses chromaticism to shift back down to ninth position and resolve in the same spot where it began.

TIP: Use a three-string index-finger barre at fret 9 for the phrase in measures 1–2, hammering onto fret 12 with your pinky. In measure 3, use your index and ring fingers for the 12th- and 14th-fret double stops, respectively. For the descending chromatic line, use a combination of your index, middle, and ring fingers, high (string) to low, shifting the shape down one fret at a time.

 Key of E

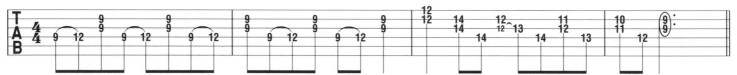

 Key of G

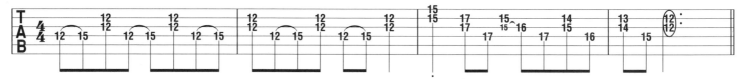

 Key of A

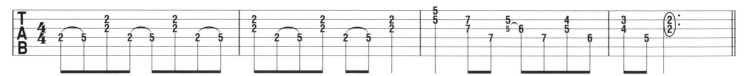

 Key of C

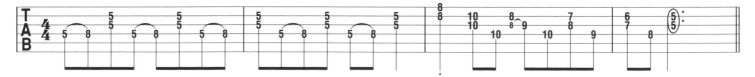

LICK 10
Crossing Blue Lines

MUSICAL STYLE: *Jazz Fusion*

SOUNDS LIKE: *Robben Ford*

OVERVIEW: This phrase is based on the same scale pattern that began Lick 9, with a few extra notes thrown in for added color. The entire phrase is performed in ninth position and in an eighth-note-triplet rhythm, pulling its notes from a combination of the major and minor pentatonic scales.

TIP: Play the trio of notes on beat 2 of measure 2 with your pinky, middle, and ring fingers, respectively, followed by your pinky for the final note of the phrase. If this feels too awkward, try shifting your fret hand up to 10th position and playing the notes in this order: ring, index, and middle.

 Key of E

♩ = 100

E7

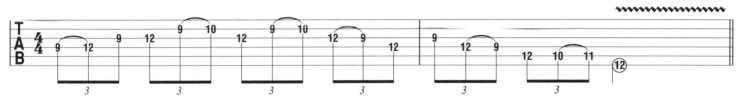

 Key of G

♩ = 100

G7

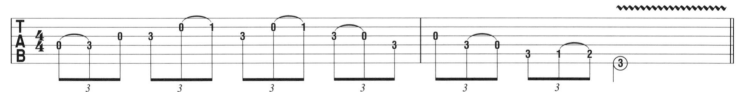

 Key of A

♩ = 100

A7

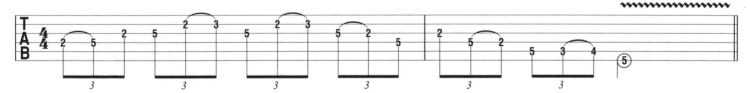

 Key of D

♩ = 100

D7

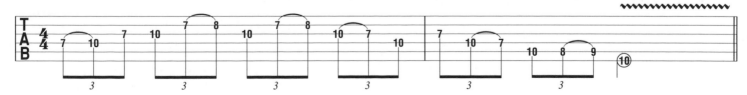

LICK 11
Deep Pull-Offs

MUSICAL STYLE: Neoclassical

SOUNDS LIKE: Ritchie Blackmore

OVERVIEW: Part metal and part classical music, the neoclassical genre was pioneered by former Deep Purple guitarist Ritchie Blackmore, and this lick is quite representative of his style. The phrase features a series of major and minor triads performed as pull-off figures along strings 1–2. The result is a minor-key chord progression, Gm–Cm–D–Gm (i–iv–V–i), commonly found in classical music.

TIP: Use a two-string index-finger barre (fret 8) for the Cm shape, moving it up to fret 10 for the D shape. Be aware, however, that you'll need to extend your pinky an extra fret for the high F♯ note to account for the D triad's major tonality.

 Key of G Minor

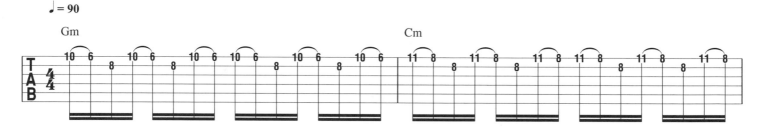

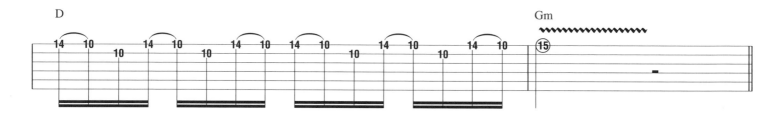

 Key of A Minor

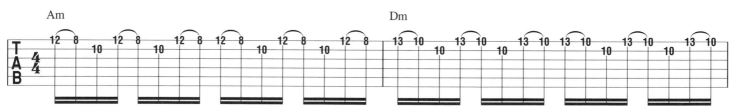

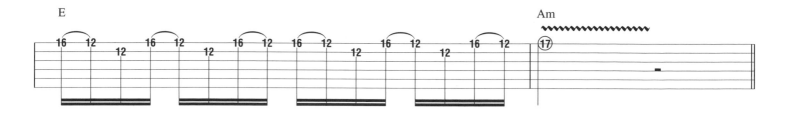

Key of C Minor

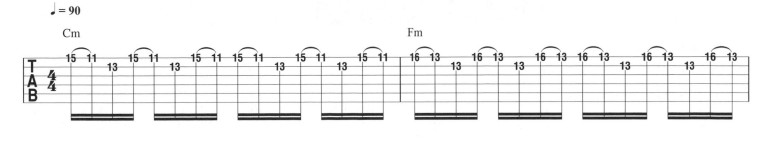

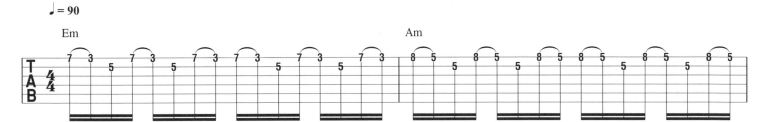

Key of E Minor

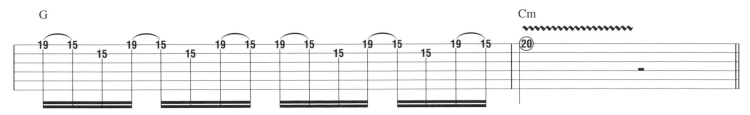

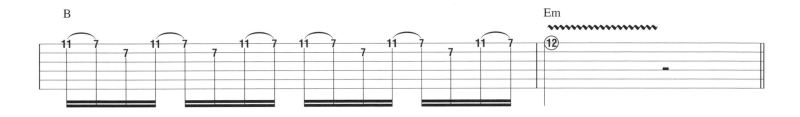

LICK 12
Delta Double Stops

MUSICAL STYLE: Blues

SOUNDS LIKE: Muddy Waters

OVERVIEW: This double-stop turnaround lick is indicative of Muddy Waters's music. Played here (initially) in the key of E, the phrase starts with triplet double stops composed of the I (E7) chord's 5th (B) and ♭7th (D) before shifting down to open position for a chromatic walk-up to the V (B7) chord.

TIP: Perform the double stops with your ring and middle fingers on strings 3 and 2, respectively. This will put your hand in an advantageous position for performing the remainder of the lick, especially when you play it in other keys.

 Key of E

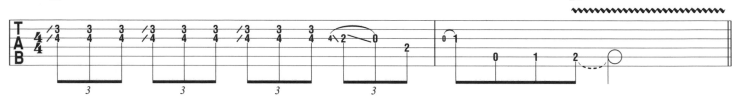

 Key of A

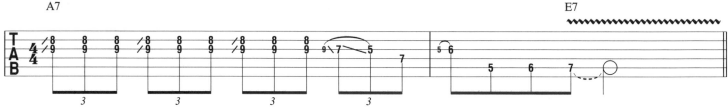

 Key of B

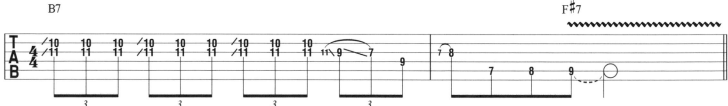

 Key of D

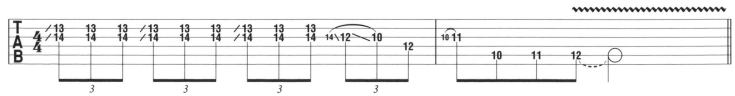

LICK 13
Diary of a Tapman

MUSICAL STYLE: Neoclassical/Metal

SOUNDS LIKE: Randy Rhoads

OVERVIEW: The harmony used here (Am–E) is similar to that used in Lick 11, only this one covers just two chords (i and V) instead of three (i, iv, and V). Also, the triads in this figure are articulated with a combination of right-hand tapping and pull-offs.

TIP: You can use either your pick hand's index or middle finger to execute the tapping. Try both and go with the one that feels most natural to you. That being said, one thing you'll want to consider is your pick—specifically, where you'll be holding it while you tap. Although this phrase is performed exclusively with tapping, this won't always be the case.

Key of A Minor

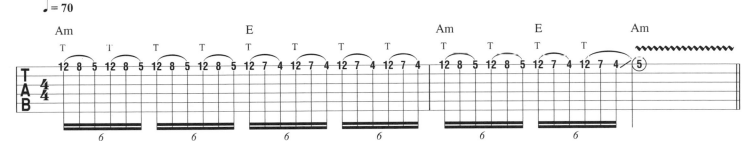

Key of B Minor

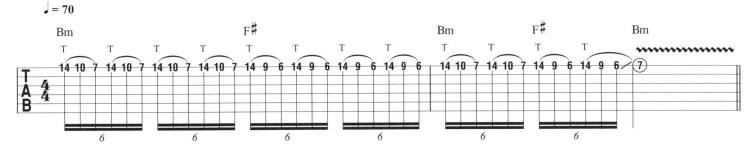

Key of E Minor

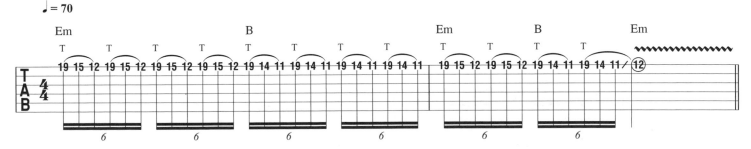

Key of F# Minor

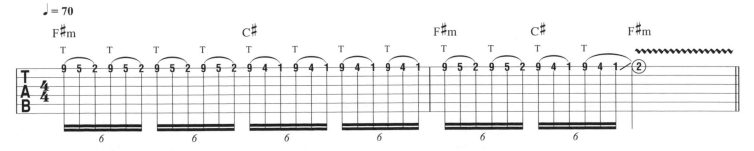

LICK 14
Django Unrestrained

MUSICAL STYLE: *Jazz*

SOUNDS LIKE: Django Reinhardt

OVERVIEW: Don't let the chord symbols scare you away; this lick is actually fairly easy to perform. The entire phrase is composed of a diminished seventh-chord arpeggio played in a pattern that descends the strings in groups of 3. The two-note pattern on each string moves down the neck one fret at a time, with the only exception being strings 2 and 3, where it jumps two frets due to the guitar's unique tuning.

TIP: Use alternate picking (down-up-down-up, etc.) throughout, starting with a downstroke.

Key of G Minor

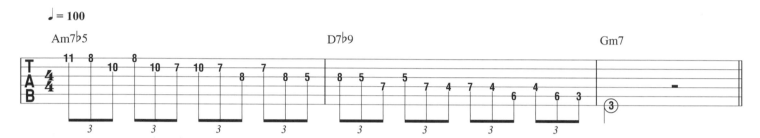

Key of B♭ Minor

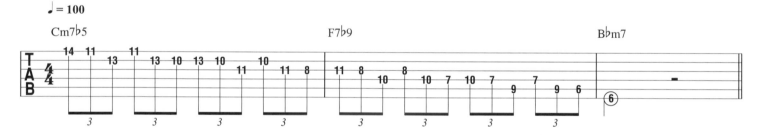

Key of D♭ Minor

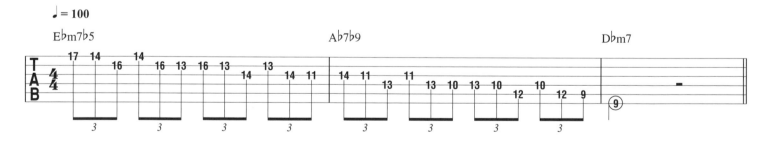

Key of E Minor

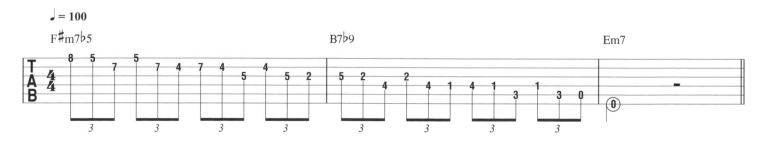

LICK 15
Double-Stop Rock

MUSICAL STYLE: Early Rock 'n' Roll

SOUNDS LIKE: Chuck Berry

OVERVIEW: Although Chuck's bending lick (see Lick 5) might be the most oft-repeated lick in the blues-rock lexicon, this one isn't far behind! Indeed, the three-note pickup is a case study in rock guitar in and of itself. The notes are mostly rooted in the A Mixolydian mode (A–B–C♯–D–E–F♯–G), with the double stops played in a three-against-four rhythm, also known as a *polyrhythm*. In this case, the double stops are performed in groups of 3 over a four-beat pulse (i.e., 4/4 time).

TIP: It's imperative that you slide into the first double stop of each group of 3. Without the slides, the lick loses its syncopation, which is the essence of the line.

 Key of A

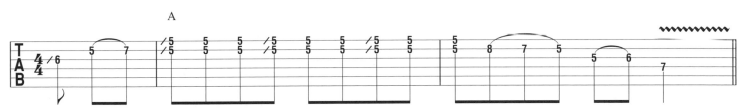

 **Key of D**

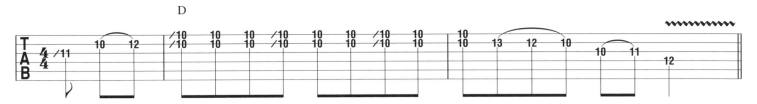

 Key of E

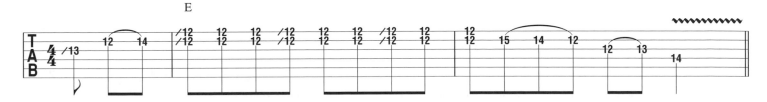

 Key of G

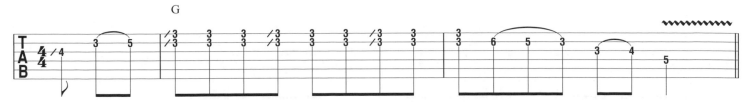

LICK 16
Flatpicker's Delight

MUSICAL STYLE: Bluegrass

SOUNDS LIKE: Tony Rice

OVERVIEW: No key is more prominent in bluegrass than G major, and that's the key of this first example. Although Tony Rice probably would pick every note of this lick, hammer-ons are included here to make its performance easier. The notes are mostly derived from the G major pentatonic scale, with one exception—the ♭3rd. This combination of notes is sometimes referred to as the G major blues scale (G–A–B♭–B–D–E) due to its inclusion of both a major and minor 3rd.

TIP: Use your middle finger for all notes on fret 3, and your index finger for the notes on fret 2. Use a similar strategy (assigning one finger per fret) for the licks in other keys.

 Key of G

 Key of A

 Key of C

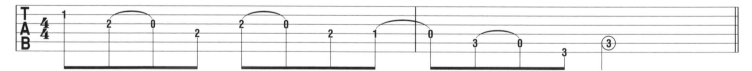

 Key of D

LICK 17
Full Haus

MUSICAL STYLE: *Jazz*

SOUNDS LIKE: Wes Montgomery

OVERVIEW: Though Wes Montgomery could play smokin' single-note lines, the technique he's most closely associated with is *octaves*, which involve playing two notes simultaneously. An octave is a musical interval consisting of 12 half steps (frets). When you move from one note to another that is 12 half steps away, you arrive at its octave. It's the same pitch, just one octave higher or lower, depending on which direction you move. The lick below features octave shapes exclusively and combines minor and major tonalities for a line that would feel right at home in a 12-bar jazz blues.

TIP: As you strum, use the underside of your fret-hand index finger to mute the string that separates the fretted pitches. For a true Wes tone, try brushing the strings with your pick-hand thumb in lieu of strumming with a pick.

 Key of A

 Key of C

Key of F

 Key of G

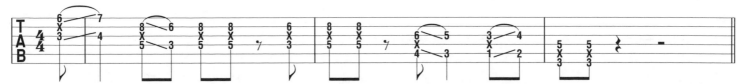

LICK 18
Gatton After It!

MUSICAL STYLE: Country

SOUNDS LIKE: Danny Gatton

OVERVIEW: This double-stop phrase should look somewhat familiar, as it borrows elements from Lick 9. What gives this phrase its character is the use of repetition and rhythmic displacement. In this case, when the phrase from measure 1 is repeated in measure 2, it is moved (displaced) from its original location, coming in on the "and" of beat 1 rather than on the downbeat of beat 2.

TIP: These types of licks are most easily executed with hybrid picking; that is, with a combination of your pick and fingers. Pluck the notes on string 4 with your pick, using your middle and ring fingers to grab the double stops.

 Key of A

 Key of C

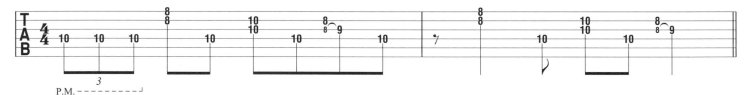

 Key of E

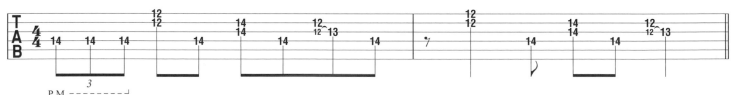

 Key of G

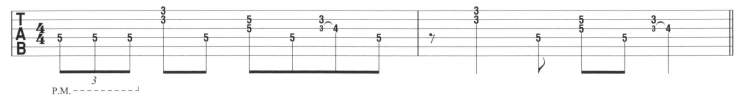

LICK 19
Hendrixian Hammer-Ons

MUSICAL STYLE: R&B

SOUNDS LIKE: Jimi Hendrix

OVERVIEW: This lick, played over an E–D–A (V–IV–I) progression, is a good example of Jimi's exemplary lead/rhythm playing, a style he co-opted from R&B/soul icon Curtis Mayfield. Although it might not be readily apparent due to the abundance of slides and hammer-ons, each one-bar phrase is derived from a fifth-string (E and D) or sixth-string (A) barre-chord shape.

TIP: In measure 3, wrap your thumb over the top of the neck to fret the sixth-string A note at fret 5. This will make it easier to execute the double-stop slide. Also, grab the A note on the high E string with your ring finger after sliding back down strings 3 and 2 with your index and middle fingers, respectively.

 Key of A

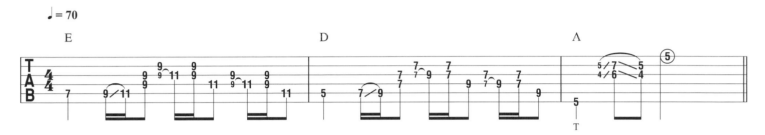

 **Key of D**

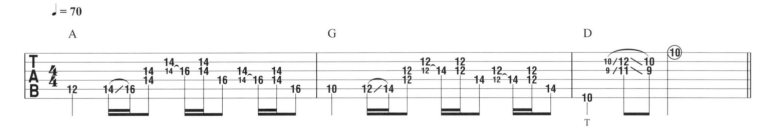

 **Key of E**

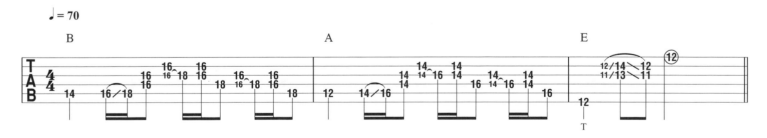

 **Key of G**

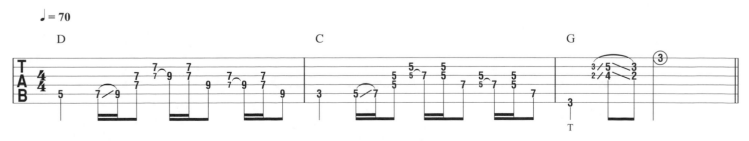

LICK 20
If 3 Was 4

MUSICAL STYLE: Blues Rock

SOUNDS LIKE: Jimi Hendrix

OVERVIEW: The phrasing found in this lick is similar to the double stops in Lick 15 in that the repetitive, three-note bend/hammer-on figure is played in a three-against-four rhythm. The entire example is performed in the first pattern (box 1) of the E minor pentatonic scale.

TIP: Count the 16th notes like so: "one-ee-and-uh, two-ee-and-uh," etc. The first bend comes in on "one," the second on the "uh" of beat 1, the third on the "and" of beat 2, and the fourth on the "ee" of beat 3. Listen to the accompanying audio to get a better feel for this syncopation.

 **Key of E**

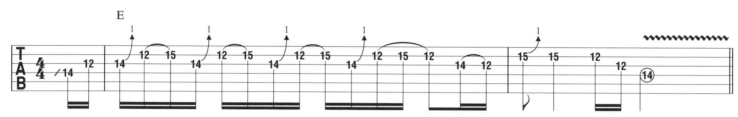

 Key of F#

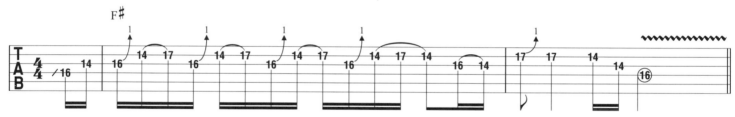

 Key of A

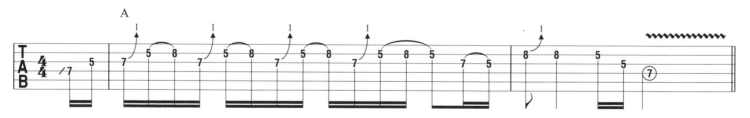

Key of B

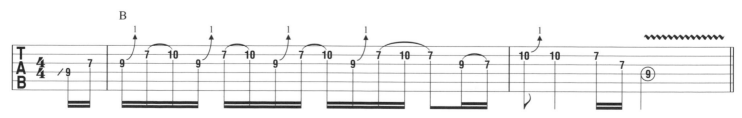

LICK 21
Invoking the 5th

MUSICAL STYLE: Hard Rock

SOUNDS LIKE: Steve Vai

OVERVIEW: Few rock guitarists have a more identifiable sound than Steve Vai. One way Vai achieves his distinctive sound is via his unconventional methods for applying certain intervals. For example, instead of strumming the 5ths in this lick as power chords like most guitarists would do, he plays the shapes as individual notes moved swiftly up the fretboard, with each new shape starting on the top note of the previous one (after a quick grace-note slide).

TIP: Use your index and ring fingers for the first three intervals, switching to an index-middle combo for strings 3–2. For the two intervals on strings 2–1, go back to your index and ring fingers.

 **Key of B**

♩ = 120

B7sus4

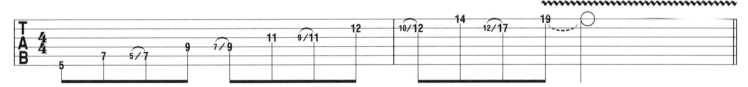

 **Key of C♯**

♩ = 120

C♯7sus4

 **Key of G**

♩ = 120

G7sus4

 **Key of A**

♩ = 120

A7sus4

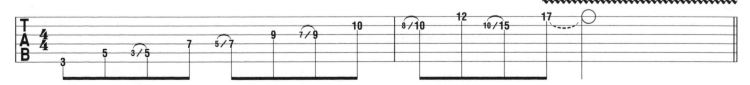

LICK 22
Key of G Flatt

MUSICAL STYLE: Bluegrass

SOUNDS LIKE: Lester Flatt

OVERVIEW: This is—hands down—the most played lick in bluegrass. Known as a "G run," the phrase follows the shape of an open G chord, using notes from the G major blues scale (G–A–B♭–B–D–E). The juxtaposition of major (B) and minor (B♭) tonalities is a vital sound of both bluegrass and country guitar.

TIP: The presence of hammer-ons might cause you to rush the lick, so concentrate on playing each note in time. For proper articulation, listen to the accompanying audio example.

 Key of G

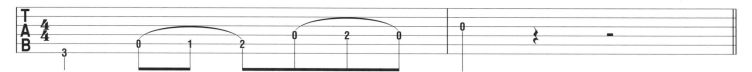

 Key of A

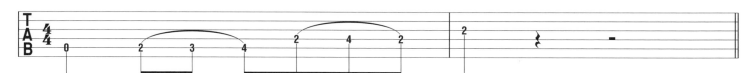

 Key of C

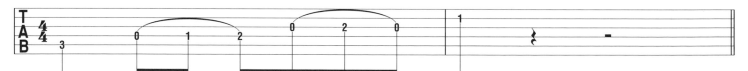

 Key of D

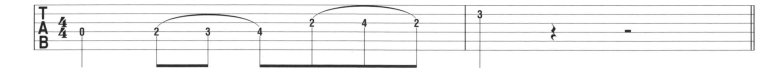

LICK 23
King of Bends

MUSICAL STYLE: Blues

SOUNDS LIKE: Albert King

OVERVIEW: Like B.B. (Lick 4), Albert King has his own "box" on the neck of the guitar due to his penchant to play from this one particular pattern. The "Albert King box" is an upper extension of box 1 of the minor pentatonic scale, with notes straddling both box 1 and box 2. The lick below exploits the Albert box and features a plethora of bends—Albert's favorite technique!

TIP: Slide into the lick with your middle finger. This will put your other fingers in an advantageous position for the rest of the lick.

 **Key of A**

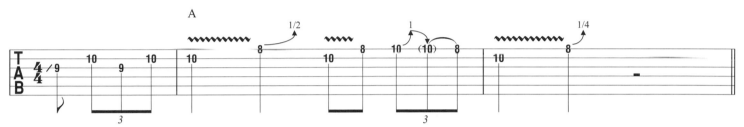

 **Key of D**

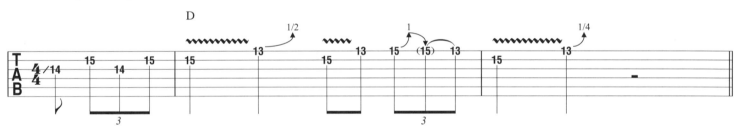

 **Key of E**

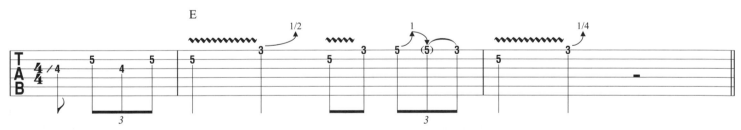

 **Key of G**

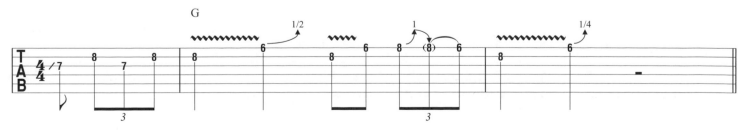

LICK 24
Kirk, Tap It

MUSICAL STYLE: Metal/Hard Rock

SOUNDS LIKE: Kirk Hammett

OVERVIEW: This type of tapping phrase is a favorite of Metallica guitarist Kirk Hammett. It's similar to Lick 13 in that the three-note sequences spell out major and minor triads. What separates this phrase from the previous example, however, is that, while tapping out its Em–C–Bm–G (i–VI–v–III) progression, this one shifts from string 1 to string 2.

TIP: If you examine this lick closely, you'll notice that the fret-hand fingers never move; the pinky and index fingers stay planted on frets 15 and 12, respectively. Therefore, most of your attention can be focused on shifting your tapping finger and on making the transition from string 1 to string 2.

 Key of E Minor

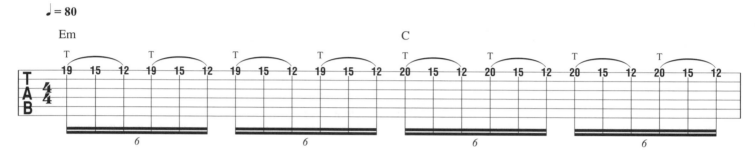

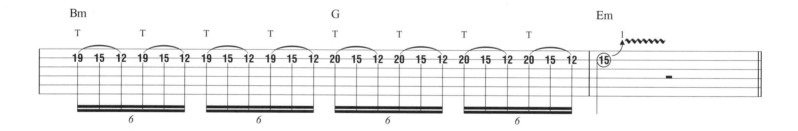

 Key of F♯ Minor

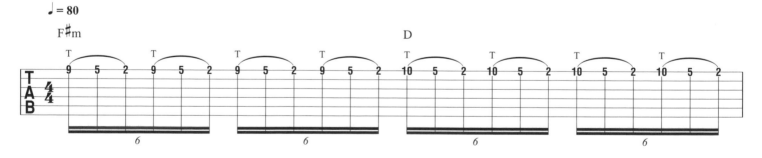

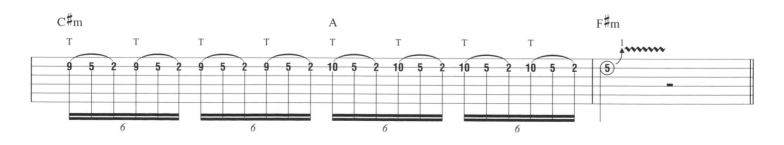

Key of A Minor

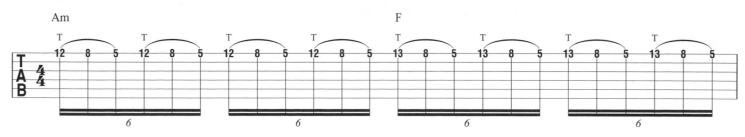

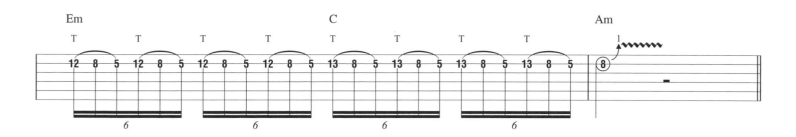

Key of B Minor

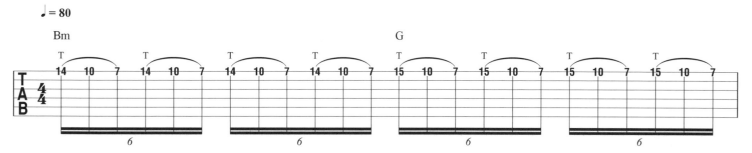

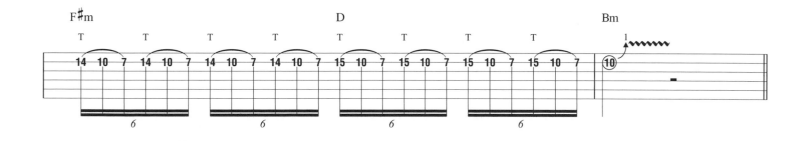

LICK 25
Lone Star Alteration

MUSICAL STYLE: Blues

SOUNDS LIKE: Stevie Ray Vaughan

OVERVIEW: It's hard to pick one thing that made Stevie Ray Vaughan so great, but from strictly a guitar-playing perspective, his ability to insert the ♭9th alteration into his lines is definitely one. An *alteration* is a note that falls outside the underlying chord (or scale)—that is, it's been "altered." In this example, the chord is G7 and the alteration is the ♭9th, A♭, which is found in the 16th-note triplet (fret 4, string 1). The addition of the ♭9th gives the line a brief G7♭9 (an altered chord) sound.

TIP: Don't miss the quarter-step bend on beat 3. This slight upward nudge makes a huge difference with respect to giving the line a genuine blues flavor.

 Key of G

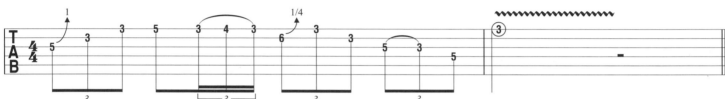

 Key of A

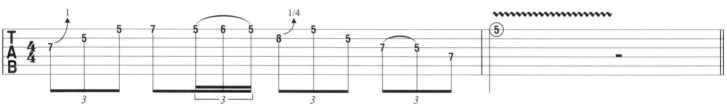

 Key of C

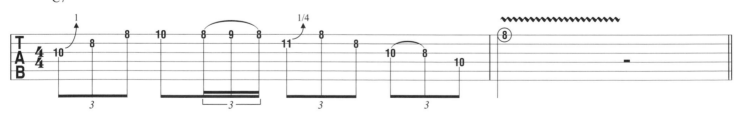

 Key of E

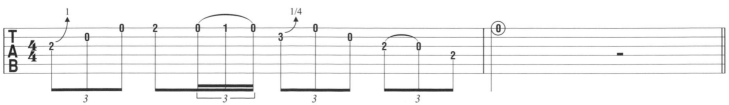

LICK 26
Lynch Mode

MUSICAL STYLE: Hard Rock

SOUNDS LIKE: George Lynch

OVERVIEW: The former Dokken guitarist has always been known for his bluesy yet exotic-sounding leads, and this lick doesn't disappoint. This two-bar phrase is derived from the A Lydian mode (A–B–C#–D#–E–F#–G#) and features tapping-finger slides throughout.

TIP: Have your fret-hand fingers positioned at their correct frets before starting the lick: index finger at fret 6, ring finger at fret 8, and pinky at fret 9. And use your middle finger for the lick's final note, A (fret 7, string 4). To sound this note, you can either pluck it with your pick or hammer onto it with your middle finger.

 Key of A

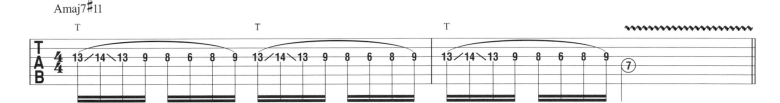

 Key of B

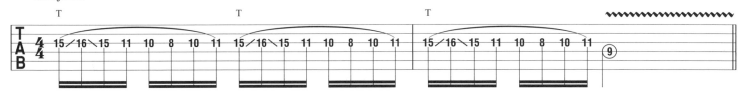

Key of E

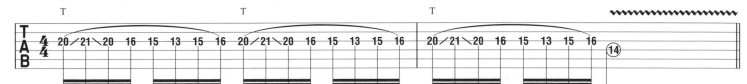

 Key of F#

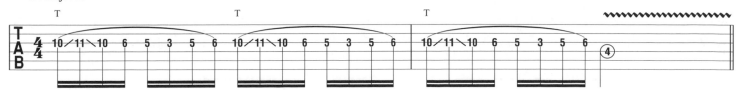

LICK 27
Major Betts

MUSICAL STYLE: Southern Rock/Country

SOUNDS LIKE: Dickey Betts

OVERVIEW: Betts is known for his ability to construct long, flowing lines from the major pentatonic scale (1–2–3–5–6). Although this lick is only three measures long, it is a good representation of the former Allman Brothers Band guitarist's style. Similar to Lick 3, the phrase starts with a pedal-steel-style bend and then proceeds to descend the G major pentatonic scale.

TIP: Perform the bend with your ring finger, reinforced with your middle and index, and grab the note on string 1 (D) with your pinky. This will put your fret hand in an advantageous position for the rest of the lick.

 **Key of G**

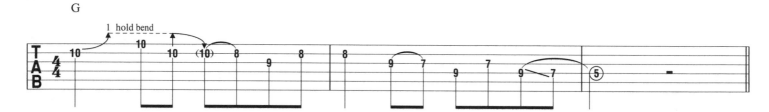

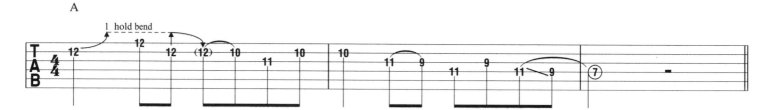 **Key of A**

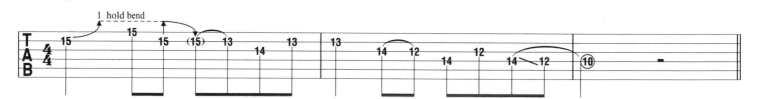 **Key of C**

 **Key of D**

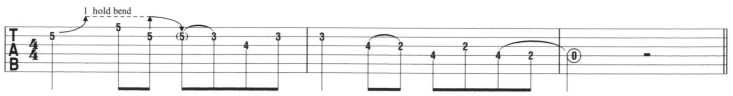

LICK 28
Mason Pickin' Line

MUSICAL STYLE: Country

SOUNDS LIKE: Brent Mason

OVERVIEW: Nashville session pro Brent Mason is one of the most recorded guitarists in country music history. And there's a reason for that: in a town full of fierce flatpickers, Mason is one of the fiercest! This lick is indicative of the way Mason incorporates open strings while outlining major or dominant seventh chords. Like some of the other country licks in this book, the notes are derived from the major blues scale.

TIP: Perform the first hammer-on with your index and ring fingers. This will free up your middle finger for the subsequent pull-off on string 3.

 Key of A

♩ = 140

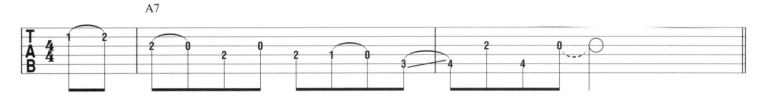

 Key of D

♩ = 140

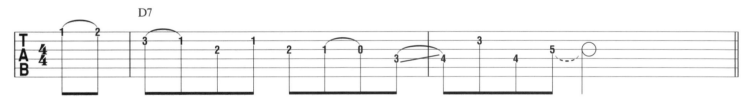

 Key of E

♩ = 140

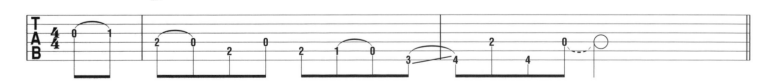

 Key of G

♩ = 140

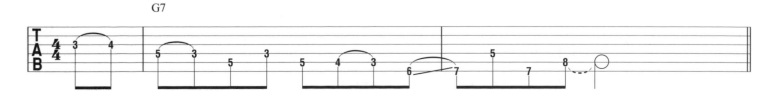

LICK 29
Mayer of Sweepville

MUSICAL STYLE: Blues Rock

SOUNDS LIKE: John Mayer

OVERVIEW: John Mayer has never been shy about discussing his influences, and one of his biggest is blues icon Stevie Ray Vaughan. This two-bar phrase in C minor is straight out of the Mayer playbook, but it has shades of SRV, as well. All of the notes are taken from the C minor pentatonic scale, but the main focus here is on the economy picking, also known as "sweep" picking.

TIP: Pick each of the double stops with a downstroke, hammering onto the strings with your ring finger. After the hammer-on, use a single upstroke to sweep through the 16th-note triplet, quickly repositioning your ring finger to the last note of the triplet (pinky for the last triplet).

 Key of C Minor

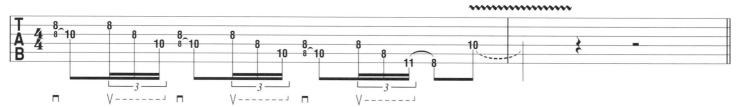

 Key of F Minor

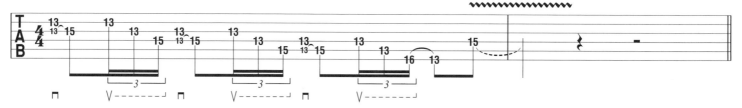

 Key of G Minor

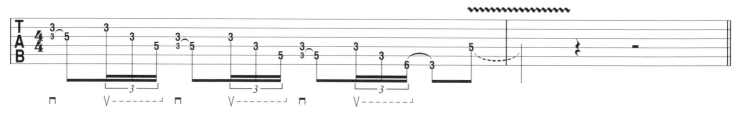

 Key of A Minor

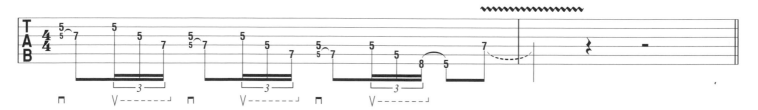

LICK 30
Minor Scale with a Major Problem

MUSICAL STYLE: Hard Rock

SOUNDS LIKE: Angus Young

OVERVIEW: The signature sound of the blues and blues-based rock is the juxtaposition of minor and major tonalities. AC/DC guitarist Angus Young is a master of blending these sounds in his leads, as the example below demonstrates. Here, a one-bar phrase is constructed from the A minor pentatonic scale and then shifted down three frets to the A *major* pentatonic scale. The result is pure Angus!

TIP: On beat 3 of each measure, voice the notes residing on the same fret with a ring-finger barre, gently rolling it back and forth as you move between strings 4 and 3.

Key of A

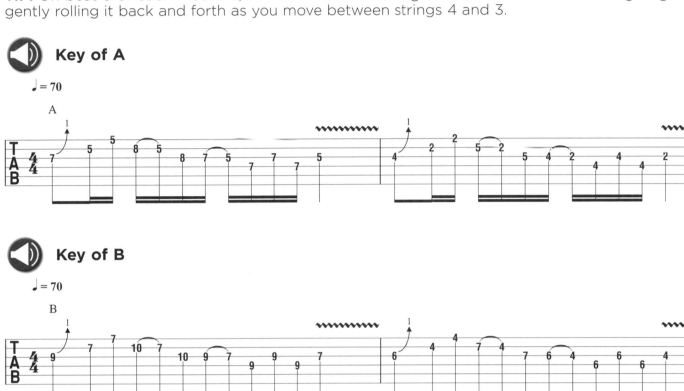

Key of B

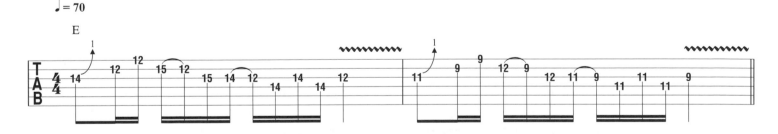

Key of E

Key of F♯

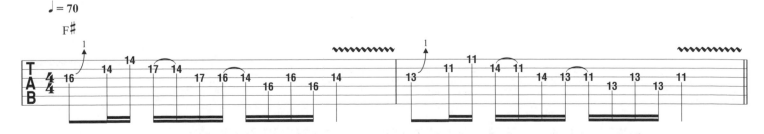

LICK 31
The Mixolydian Potato Head Groove Thing

MUSICAL STYLE: Hard Rock

SOUNDS LIKE: Joe Satriani

OVERVIEW: If there's an overarching theme to Joe Satriani's playing, it's *legato*. Whether it's finger taps, hammer-ons, or pull-offs, Satch's lines have always had a fluidity that escapes most guitarists. The lick below is an example of how Satch might attack a dominant seventh chord. Derived entirely from the B Mixolydian mode (B–C#–D#–E–F#–G#–A), the descending line features a six-note pattern that is repeated on each new string on its way to the root (B) on fret 9 of string 4.

TIP: Practice the six-note patterns on each string individually until they feel comfortable. Then attempt the whole lick, starting at a slow tempo (e.g., 40 BPM).

 Key of B

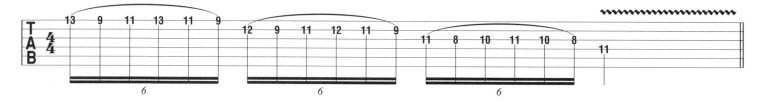

 Key of C#

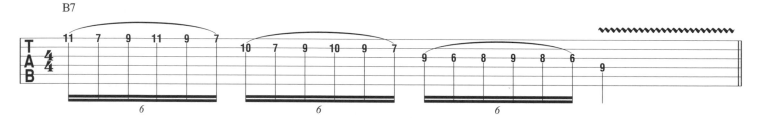

 Key of E

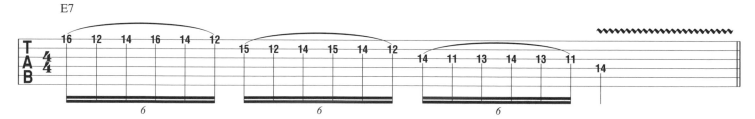

 Key of F#

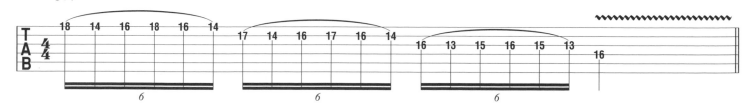

LICK 32
Moore Bends

MUSICAL STYLE: Blues Rock

SOUNDS LIKE: Gary Moore

OVERVIEW: Blues-rock guitarist Gary Moore was the original "shredder." Before the likes of Yngwie Malmsteen, Paul Gilbert, and Steve Vai became household names in the 1980s, Moore was melting faces as a member of Thin Lizzy and, later, as a solo artist. But the Irish guitarist wasn't all flash; he played with deep emotion, as well. The lick below captures both aspects of Moore's playing over the course of two bars. The entire phrase is rooted in the A minor pentatonic scale and played in a repetitive rhythm consisting of eighth notes and 16th-note triplets.

TIP: Use the following prompt to count this rhythm: "*one*-trip-uh-let, *two*-trip-uh-let, *three*-trip-uh-let, *four*-trip-uh-let."

Key of A

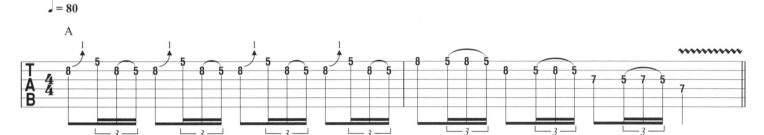

Key of D

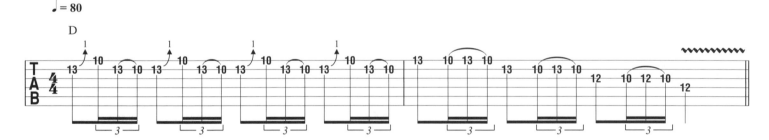

Key of E

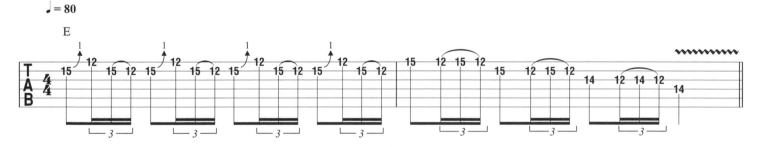

Key of G

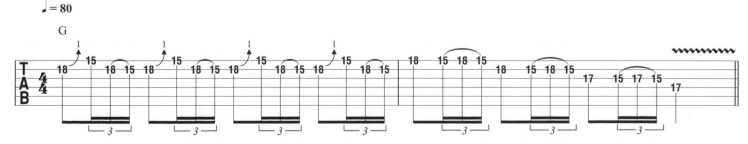

LICK 33
Mr. 335 Plays a 5-4-1

MUSICAL STYLE: Jazz Fusion

SOUNDS LIKE: Larry Carlton

OVERVIEW: This turnaround lick is played in true Larry Carlton fashion: Rather than tackle the V (E) chord and IV (D) chord with notes from pattern 1 of their relative minor pentatonic scale like most guitarists would do, this phrase instead plays out of E and D minor triad shapes on strings 1–3 and features minor 3rd-to-major 3rd bends. Then, to color the line a bit jazzier, the 6th (F#) is incorporated in measure 3 (over the A chord) in place of the more common ♭7th (G).

TIP: After using your index and middle fingers to play the C-to-C# hammer-on that bridges measures 2–3, use a ring-index combo for the 7th-fret A and 4th-fret F#, respectively, on string 4.

 Key of A

 Key of D

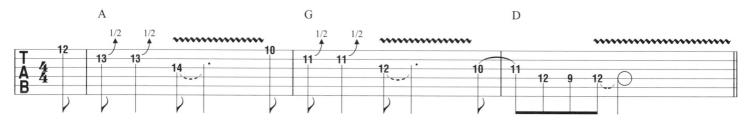

 Key of E

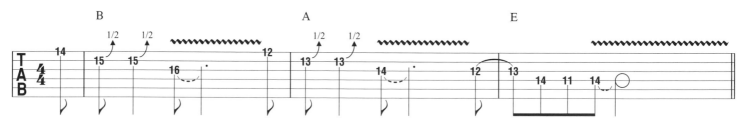

 Key of G

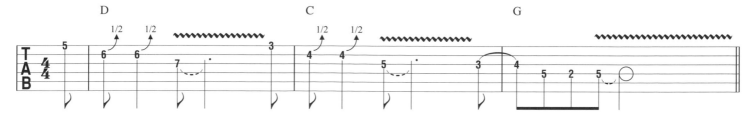

LICK 34
Page Pull-Offs

MUSICAL STYLE: Hard Rock

SOUNDS LIKE: Jimmy Page

OVERVIEW: Page's greatest gifts to the rock community are the titanic riffs he wrote as a member of Led Zeppelin, but a close second are his contributions to lead guitar playing. In fact, Page's approach to pull-offs forever changed the way rock guitarists would use the technique, especially within the confines of the minor pentatonic scale. The lick below is representative of Page's style. It uses notes from the A minor pentatonic scale for fast, repetitive pull-offs on the top two strings.

TIP: Rather than shifting your index finger back and forth between string 1 and string 2 at fret 5 (which is impossible at this speed), use a small, two-string barre.

 Key of A Minor

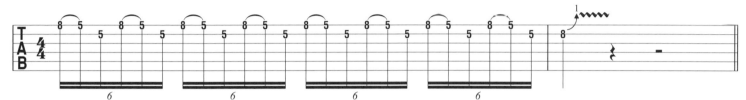

 Key of B Minor

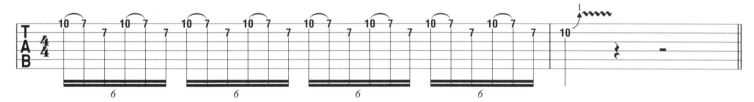

 Key of E Minor

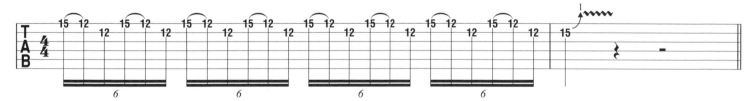

 Key of F♯ Minor

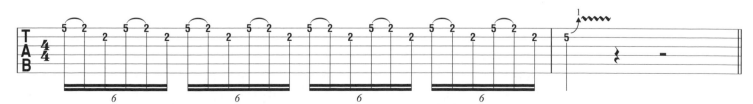

LICK 35
Paisley's Pentatonic Approach

MUSICAL STYLE: Country

SOUNDS LIKE: Brad Paisley

OVERVIEW: Country guitarists love them some major pentatonic licks, and that includes superstar Brad Paisley. This lick is rooted in C major pentatonic (C–D–E–G–A) and features a pair of interesting bends. The first one is a whole-step bend from D to E (the 3rd of the key, C). Then, on beat 1 of measure 2, the bent note is struck again and released right on the beat (i.e., as a grace note). The second bend is a bit more challenging, as it involves bending the fifth string up a whole step, which may be impossible if your guitar is strung with .011s or .012s!

TIP: For the fifth-string bend, try shifting your hand down to third position and performing it with your ring finger—reinforcing it with you middle and index—and *pulling* the string downward, toward the floor, rather than *pushing* the string upward, as you would do with bends performed on strings 1–3.

 Key of C

$\quad$ = 120

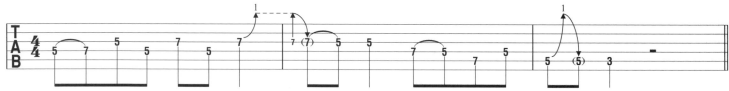

 Key of E

$\quad$ = 120

 Key of G

$\quad$ = 120

 Key of A

$\quad$ = 120

LICK 36
Pedal to the Metal

MUSICAL STYLE: Neoclassical

SOUNDS LIKE: Yngwie Malmsteen

OVERVIEW: This pedal-point lick has a distinct classical sound. Influenced by Bach, Mozart, and Paganini, among others, Yngwie is famous for employing a pedal tone on one of the treble strings and playing a descending melody below it (or vice versa). In this case, the pedal tone is the A note at fret 17 of string 1, and the melody is derived from the A harmonic minor scale (A–B–C–D–E–F–G#).

TIP: Play the pickup note, A, with an upstroke, using alternate picking for the rest of the lick. This will enable you to use a downstroke when moving to a new string, which is more efficient than using an upstroke.

 Key of A Minor

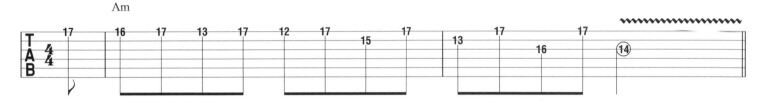

 Key of C# Minor

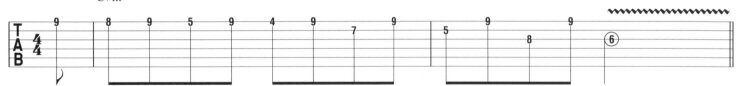

 Key of E Minor

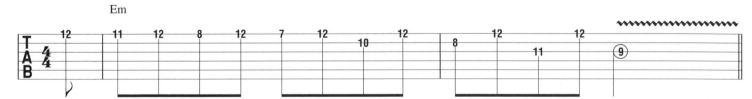

 Key of F# Minor

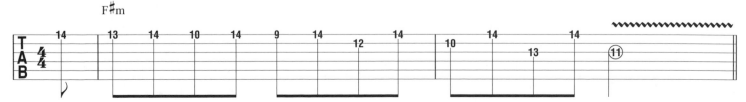

LICK 37
Randy Tones

MUSICAL STYLE: Hard Rock/Metal

SOUNDS LIKE: Randy Rhoads

OVERVIEW: When it came to guitar, Randy Rhoads could do a lot of things very well, and one such thing was playing long, fluid scale passages. The lick below is rooted in the C major scale and features both hammer-ons and pull-offs. The pattern used in this phrase involves ascending four strings, dropping down one string, and then continuing up the fretboard until it lands on its destination: the root C note at fret 8 of string 1.

TIP: This lick is actually easier than it looks. In fact, if you look closely, you'll notice that only two fingerings are used throughout. The first involves skipping a fret between each finger; the second uses a smaller stretch, with the index and middle fingers positioned on adjacent frets. Get comfortable with both fingerings before you attempt to play the entire lick.

 Key of C

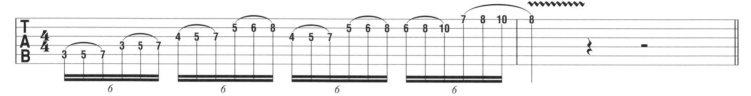

 Key of D

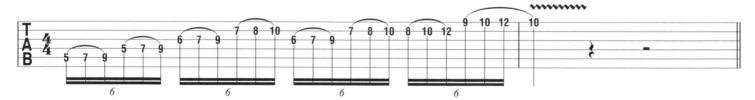

 Key of G

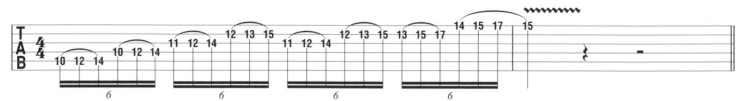

 Key of B♭

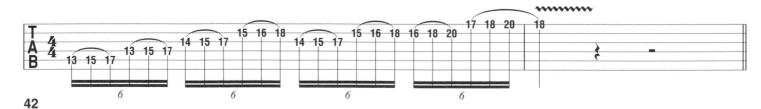

LICK 38
Shifts of Dover

MUSICAL STYLE: Blues Rock

SOUNDS LIKE: Eric Johnson

OVERVIEW: One of the signature sounds of Eric Johnson is his uncanny ability to play a seemingly endless string of notes by shifting between the various patterns (boxes) of the major or minor pentatonic scale. It results in some interesting tonalities that are unattainable by sticking to a single position. Below is a two-bar phrase that starts in pattern 1 of E minor pentatonic and then shifts downward, across two adjacent patterns.

TIP: Eric Johnson typically employs alternate picking for these types of licks, but if picking every note is too difficult at first, feel free to apply pull-offs to the note pairs on each string.

 Key of E Minor

$\quad$ = 160

Em7

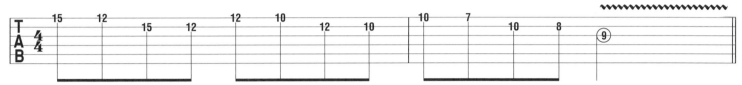

 Key of G Minor

$\quad$ = 160

Gm7

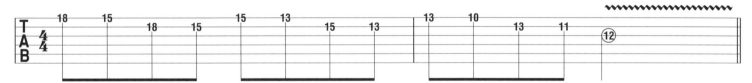

 Key of A Minor

$\quad$ = 160

Am7

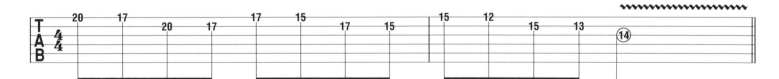

Key of C Minor

$\quad$ = 160

Cm7

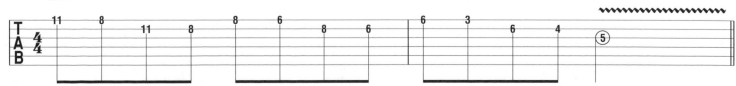

LICK 39
Slash's Sixths

MUSICAL STYLE: Hard Rock

SOUNDS LIKE: Slash

OVERVIEW: Licks like this one can be found in Guns N' Roses' "Paradise City," as well as "Beggars and Hangers On" by Slash's Snakepit. Played over a D–C–G (V–IV–I) progression, the lick revolves around minor 3rd-to-major 3rd hammer-ons and major 6th intervals. The pattern is established in measure 1 (D), transposed down a whole step for the C chord, and, finally, two-and-a-half steps (a perfect 4th) for the G chord.

TIP: Use a combination of your ring, index, and middle fingers for the three notes on string 3, quickly relocating the index finger to string 1 for the root note.

 Key of G

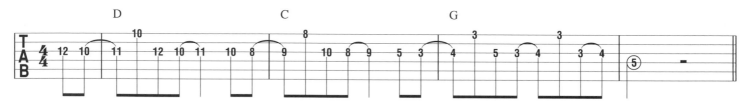

 Key of A

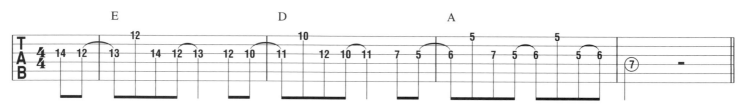

 Key of C

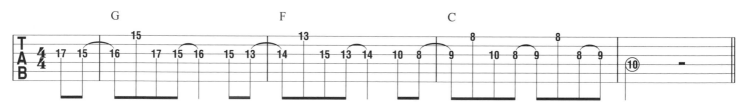

 Key of E

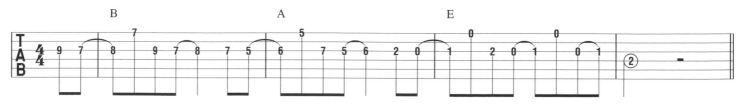

LICK 40
Slowhand Shuffle

MUSICAL STYLE: Blues Rock

SOUNDS LIKE: Eric Clapton

OVERVIEW: This lick is reminiscent of early Clapton, when he was a member of the power trio Cream. The notes are borrowed from the A minor pentatonic scale, plus the major 3rd, C# (you've seen this minor 3rd/major 3rd juxtaposition in several other licks in this book). This phrase resolves to the note E (the 5th), so it works great as a turnaround lick.

TIP: On beat 4 of measure 1, use your ring finger for the two notes at fret 7, rolling it from the finger "pad" (string 3) to the fingertip (string 4).

 Key of A

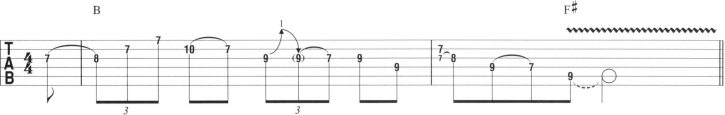

 Key of B

 Key of E

 Key of G

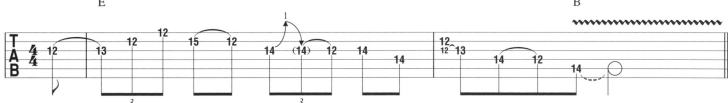

LICK 41
Smooth Pickin'

MUSICAL STYLE: Latin Rock

SOUNDS LIKE: Carlos Santana

OVERVIEW: This four-bar phrase showcases a little bit of everything Santana fans have come to love about the Latin rocker's playing: exotic sounds, fast tremolo picking, and emotive string bending. The exotic sounds are supplied by the A harmonic minor scale, and after two bars of fairly sparse phrasing, the lick ends with a flurry: When the line reaches string 2, it shifts to tremolo picking to climb the remainder of the scale, resolving to the A note at fret 17 of string 1.

TIP: The tremolo-picked notes in measures 3–4 should be picked as 16th notes. Use strict alternate picking (down-up-down-up, etc.), plucking each note four times before moving on to the next. If you're comfortable with the technique, alternate pick each note as fast as possible for the duration of each beat for a truer tremolo technique.

 Key of A Minor

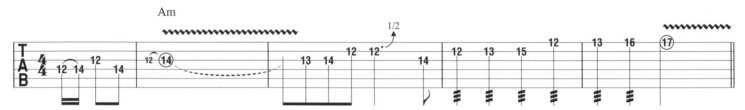

 Key of C Minor

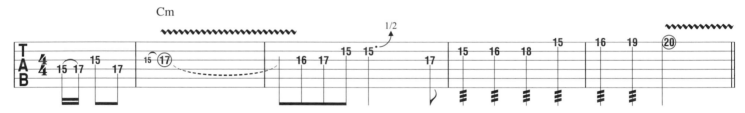

 **Key of E Minor**

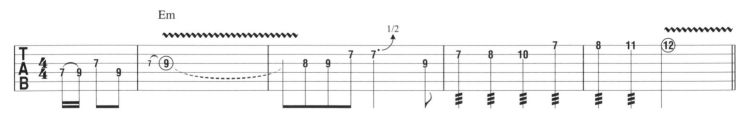

 **Key of G Minor**

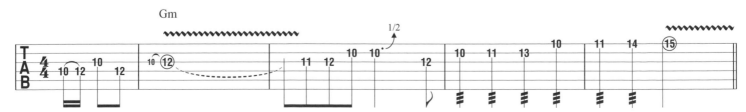

LICK 42
Stevie's Sixths

MUSICAL STYLE: R&B/Soul

SOUNDS LIKE: Steve Cropper

OVERVIEW: You learned Slash's approach to the 6th interval in Lick 39. Now let's take a look at how the great soul and R&B guitarist Steve Cropper played them. Similar to his playing on Sam and Dave's "Soul Man," this lick exemplifies how Cropper might play over a dominant seventh chord. The line begins with a shape at fret 12 that implies a C major triad (C–E–G) before making its way down to frets 8 and 6, where, again, a C triad is implied, as well as a C7 chord (C–E–G–B♭).

TIP: Begin the phrase with your middle (string 3) and ring (string 1) fingers, shifting to a middle-index combo as you approach measure 2.

 Key of C

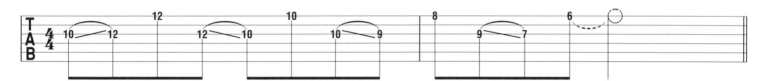

 Key of D

 Key of E

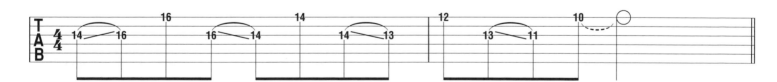

 Key of A

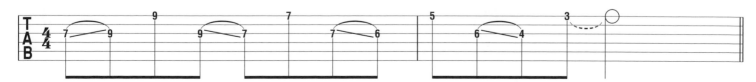

LICK 43
Sultan of Strings

MUSICAL STYLE: Rock

SOUNDS LIKE: Mark Knopfler

OVERVIEW: Although the pattern is different, the triad shapes used in this lick are similar to the ones used in Lick 11. Dire Straits guitarist/frontman Mark Knopfler is fond of using these types of shapes in his guitar solos. In fact, you can hear a similar phrase in the group's smash hit "Sultans of Swing." The lick is played over a D minor progression, Dm–Bb–C, with the arpeggio shapes adjusted or moved to accommodate each new chord.

TIP: The best right-hand strategy for this lick is to use economy picking throughout. Start with an upstroke on string 1, perform the pull-off, then continue with the upward movement, playing string 2 with an upstroke, as well. Finally, finish off the beat (pattern) with a downstroke as you return to string 1. Use this pattern, up (pull-off)-up-down, for every beat of the lick.

 Key of D Minor

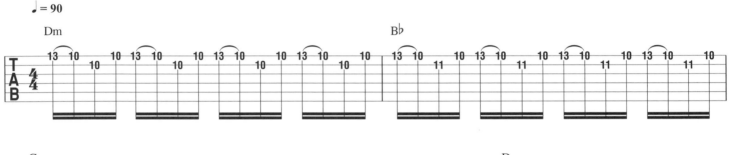

 Key of F Minor

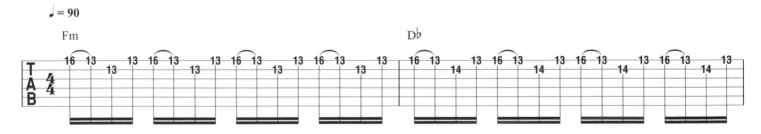

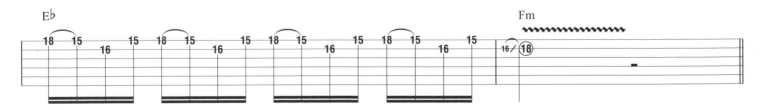

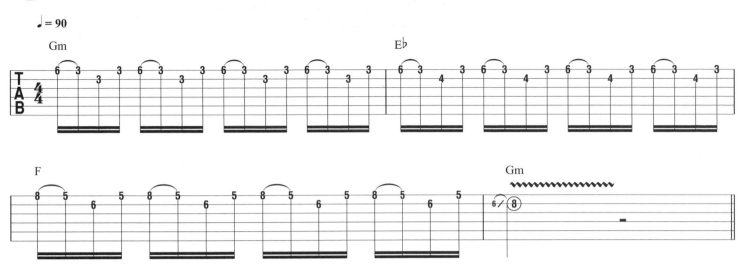

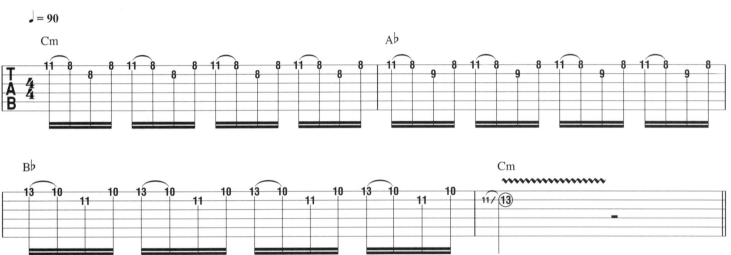

LICK 44
T-Bone's Triplets

MUSICAL STYLE: Blues

SOUNDS LIKE: T-Bone Walker

OVERVIEW: You can't do a book on licks without including one in the style of the man who was Chuck Berry's primary influence. T-Bone Walker was a trailblazer as a frontman, entertainer, and, yes, a guitar player. The lick here features repetitive triplets—a staple of T-Bone's style—that are harvested from the G minor pentatonic scale, starting with a half-step bend of the minor 3rd, Bb. Also of note is the minor 3rd-to-major 3rd (Bb-to-B) move in measure 2, which was a favorite of Walker's. This move mimics the tonalities produced by the bends, only an octave lower.

TIP: As in Lick 43, use economy picking to attack the triplets. Start with a downstroke, then switch to an upstroke and sweep through strings 1 and 2 in one motion while your index finger barres strings 1–2 at fret 3. Repeat this pattern, down-up-up, for each triplet.

 Key of G

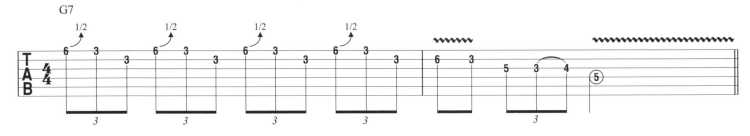

 Key of A

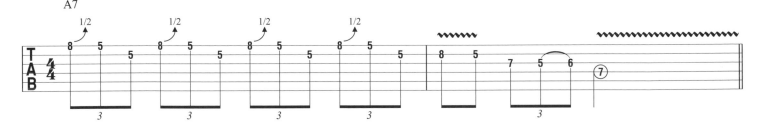

Key of C

♩ = 100 (♫ = ♪♪)

C7

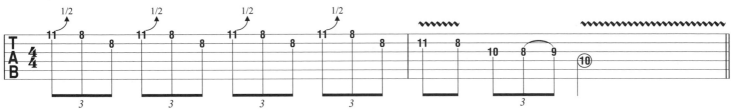

 Key of E

♩ = 100 (♫ = ♪♪)

E7

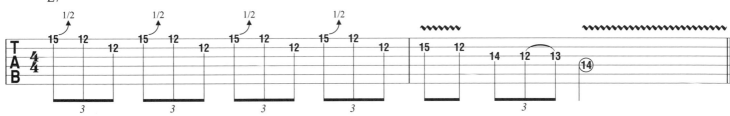

LICK 45
Tappin' Triads

MUSICAL STYLE: Hard Rock

SOUNDS LIKE: Eddie Van Halen

OVERVIEW: Of all the tapping licks you've encountered so far (Lick 13, Lick 24, and Lick 26), this one is arguably the most challenging because it involves shifting the left and right hands simultaneously as the chords change. That being said, with a little practice, it shouldn't take too long to master. The pattern here is a little different that the others: Instead of moving, in order, from the tapping finger to the pinky and index finger, this lick switches up the order of the index and pinky while spelling out the Em–D–C–D triads.

TIP: Make note of the distance your hands must travel when moving down and up the fretboard. The tapping finger moves down in whole steps (two frets). And although the left hand does the same, you must adjust your fingering to accommodate the change from a minor shape (Em) to a major one (D), which requires less of a stretch.

 **Key of E Minor**

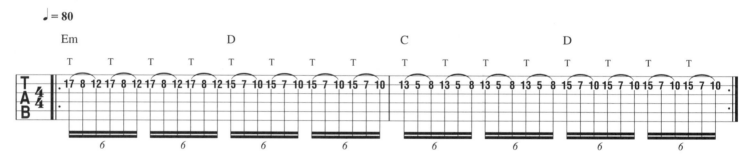

 **Key of F♯ Minor**

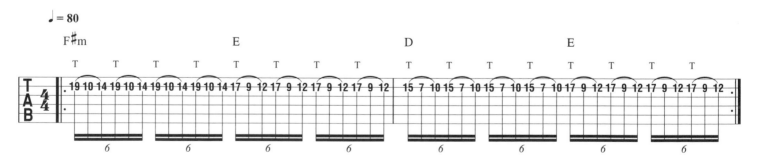

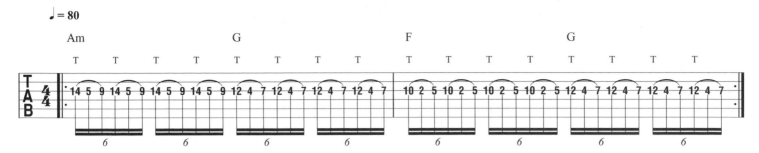

Key of A Minor

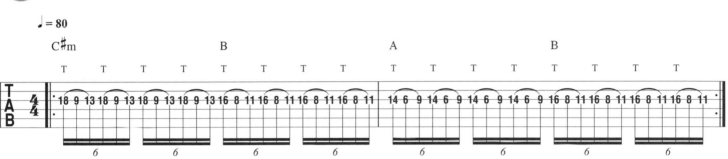

Key of C# Minor

LICK 46
Tennessee Turnaround

MUSICAL STYLE: Country

SOUNDS LIKE: Chet Atkins

OVERVIEW: You've encountered double stops in a few previous licks, but this one might be the most musical. Styled after country legend and guitar icon Chet Atkins, this lick begins in 12th position and works its way down to fifth position over the course of just two bars, outlining a C–B♭–F (V–IV–I) progression along the way. This phrase works as a great ending to a solo or song.

TIP: You can voice these double stops a few different ways, so experiment until you find a combination that works best for you. The goal should be efficiency; that is, minimal finger movement/shifting.

 Key of F

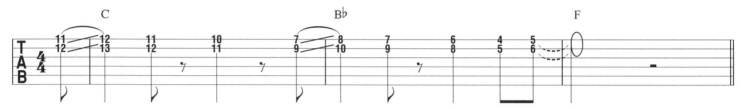

 Key of G

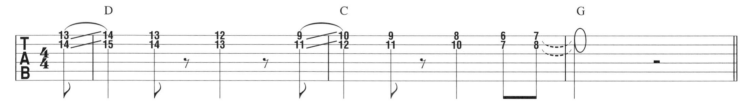

 Key of C

 Key of D

LICK 47
Triplets and Double Entendres

MUSICAL STYLE: Blues Rock

SOUNDS LIKE: Billy Gibbons

OVERVIEW: The book began with a Gibbons-style phrase (Lick 1), and now it's time to explore another one from the ZZ Top guitarist. Be careful here, as the rhythm is a bit tricky. Rather than repeating the same note sequence for each triplet, which is common practice for most guitarists, Gibbons likes to alternate just two notes to create a syncopated two-against-three feel. Genius! Melodically, all of the notes are borrowed from the C minor pentatonic scale.

TIP: In measure 1, as you alternate the G (fret 12) and Bb (fret 11) notes, be sure to count "Trip-uh-let, trip-uh-let," etc. This will help keep you from inadvertently playing the pitches as straight eighth notes.

 **Key of C**

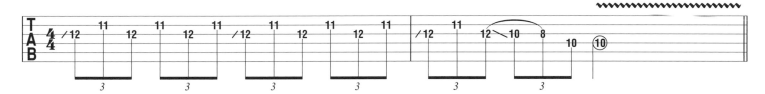

 **Key of D**

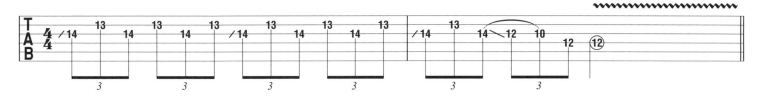

 **Key of E**

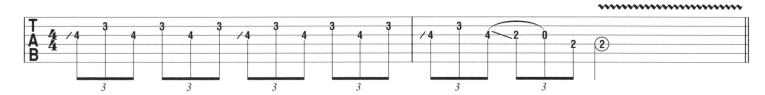

 **Key of A**

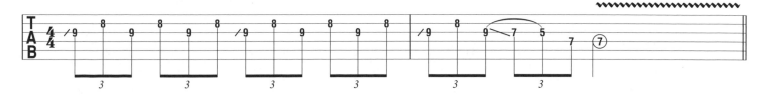

LICK 48
A Wall of Bends

MUSICAL STYLE: Rock

SOUNDS LIKE: David Gilmour

OVERVIEW: Two words best describe David Gilmour's playing style: space and taste. The Pink Floyd guitarist not only was able to say more with less but also say it at just the right time, a skill that eludes most guitarists. This lick is rooted primarily in box 1 of the D minor pentatonic scale (it briefly alludes to D Dorian in measure 2) and features a plethora of bends, including a searing two-step bend, another signature of Gilmour's playing style.

TIP: To ensure that you're hitting the right pitch during the two-step bend, find the target note on the fretboard; in this case, the E note at fret 17 of string 2. Now, before attempting the bend, fret and pick this note to hear how it sounds. Once you have the pitch in your ear, attempt the bend and try to hit that note before releasing it. Repeat these steps until the bend becomes second nature.

 Key of D Minor

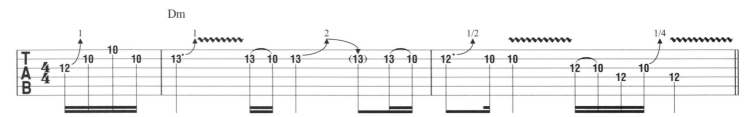

 Key of G Minor

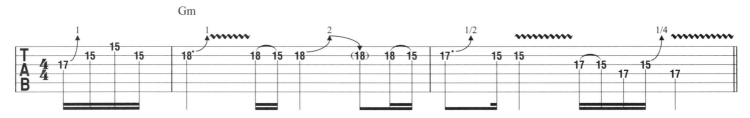

 Key of A Minor

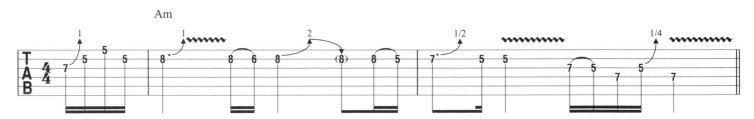

 Key of C Minor

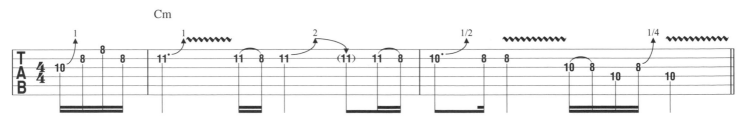

LICK 49
Winter Blues

MUSICAL STYLE: Blues Rock

SOUNDS LIKE: Johnny Winter

OVERVIEW: Similar to Gary Moore, Texas bluesman Johnny Winter was a shredder before shred was cool... well, at least mainstream. This lick is played in box 1 of the B minor pentatonic scale and features repetitive whole-step bends on string 2. The pitch of the bend matches the root of the scale, B, which is also voiced at fret 7 of string 1 immediately following the bend. This dizzying back-and-forth between bend and fretted pitch is one of Winter's signature moves.

TIP: Be sure not to overlook the quarter-step bend at the end of the lick, as it lends the phrase a bit more blues "grease." To execute this bend, pull string 3 downward, towards the floor, ever so slightly, rather than upward.

 **Key of B**

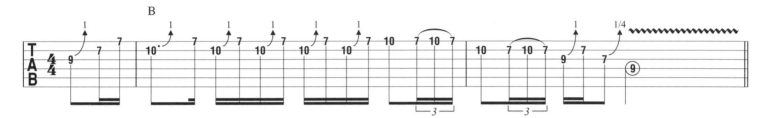

 **Key of E**

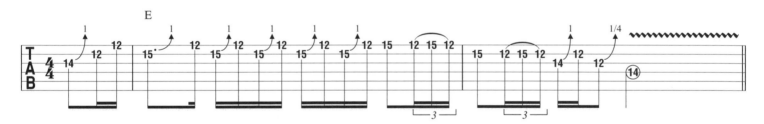

 **Key of F♯**

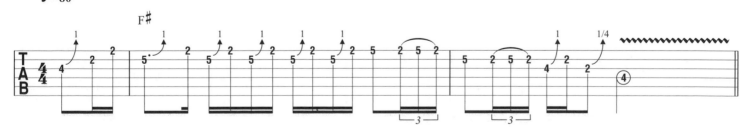

 **Key of A**

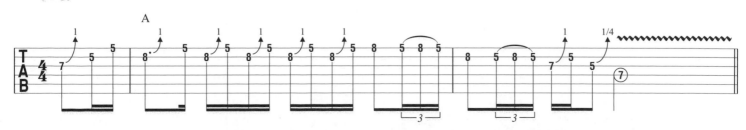

LICK 50
Wylde Pentatonics

MUSICAL STYLE: Hard Rock/Metal

SOUNDS LIKE: Zakk Wylde

OVERVIEW: Ozzy Osbourne guitarist Zakk Wylde came of age in the late 1980s, during shred's heyday. To stand out from all of the cookie-cutter shredders playing blazingly fast three-notes-per-string scale patterns, Wylde made a conscious effort to focus on two-notes-per-string pentatonic patterns. It was a wise decision, as his style is instantly recognizable. The lick below is indicative of Wylde's approach to the five-note scale. Here, the 12th-position E minor pentatonic is played in a 16th-note pattern that includes a reach up to fret 17 with the pinky. In measure 2, the lick resolves via a pattern that descends three strings, backtracks momentarily, and then continues its descent to the target pitch, E, at fret 14 of string 4.

TIP: In measure 1, use an index-ring finger combination for frets 12 and 15 so you can reach up to fret 17 with your pinky. On beat 2 of measure 2, you'll need to adjust your fingering slightly. Here, you'll want to move your ring finger to fret 14, using your pinky for the last remaining note at fret 15 (string 2).

 Key of E Minor

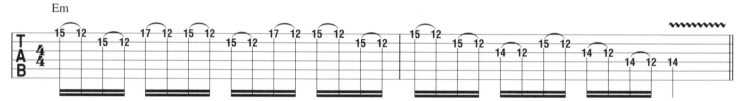

 Key of F♯ Minor

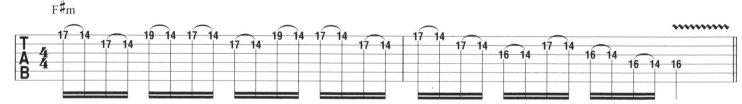

 **Key of A Minor**

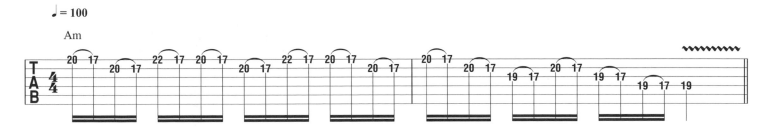

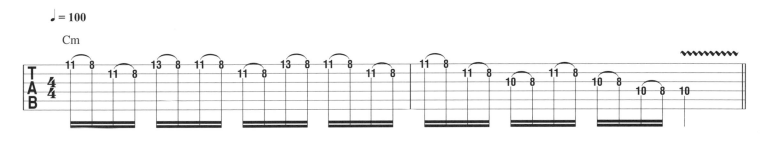 **Key of C Minor**

RHYTHM TAB LEGEND

Rhythm Tab is a form of notation that adds rhythmic values to the traditional tab staff.

TABLATURE graphically represents the guitar fingerboard. Each horizontal line represents a string, and each number represents a fret. Rhythmic values are shown using ovals, stems, and dots.

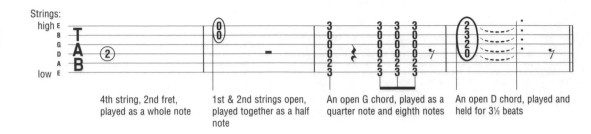

4th string, 2nd fret, played as a whole note

1st & 2nd strings open, played together as a half note

An open G chord, played as a quarter note and eighth notes

An open D chord, played and held for 3½ beats

Definitions for Special Guitar Notation

HALF-STEP BEND: Strike the note and bend up 1/2 step.

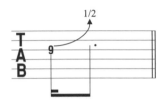

WHOLE-STEP BEND: Strike the note and bend up one step.

SLIGHT (MICROTONE) BEND: Strike the note and bend up 1/4 step.

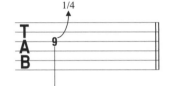

BEND AND RELEASE: Strike the note and bend up as indicated, then release back to the original note. Only the first note is struck.

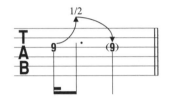

PRE-BEND: Bend the note as indicated, then strike it.

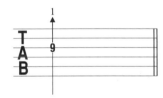

GRACE NOTE PRE-BEND AND RELEASE: Bend the note as indicated. Strike it and release the bend back to the original note.

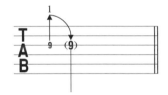

UNISON BEND: Strike the two notes simultaneously and bend the lower note up to the pitch of the higher.

HOLD BEND: While sustaining bent note, strike note on different string.

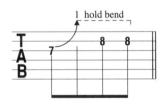

VIBRATO: The string is vibrated by rapidly bending and releasing the note with the fretting hand.

WIDE VIBRATO: The pitch is varied to a greater degree by vibrating with the fretting hand.

HAMMER-ON: Strike the first (lower) note with one finger, then sound the higher note (on the same string) with another finger by fretting it without picking.

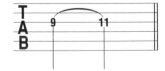

PULL-OFF: Place both fingers on the notes to be sounded. Strike the first note and without picking, pull the finger off to sound the second (lower) note.

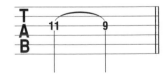

HAMMER FROM NOWHERE: Sound note(s) by hammering with fret hand finger only.

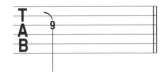

GRACE NOTE SLUR: Strike the note and immediately hammer-on (or pull-off) as indicated.

GRACE NOTE SLUR (CLUSTER): Strike the notes and immediately hammer-on (or pull-off) as indicated.

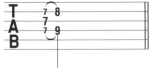

LEGATO SLIDE: Strike the first note and then slide the same fret-hand finger up or down to the second note. The second note is not struck.

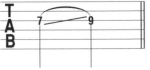

SHIFT SLIDE: Same as legato slide, except the second note is struck.

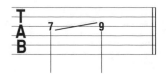

GRACE NOTE SLIDE: Quickly slide into the note from below or above.

TRILL: Very rapidly alternate between the notes indicated by continuously hammering on and pulling off.

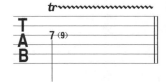

TAPPING: Hammer ("tap") the fret indicated with the pick-hand index or middle finger and pull off to the note fretted by the fret hand.

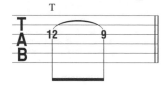

NATURAL HARMONIC: Strike the note while the fret-hand lightly touches the string directly over the fret indicated.

Harm.

PINCH HARMONIC: The note is fretted normally and a harmonic is produced by adding the edge of the thumb or the tip of the index finger of the pick hand to the normal pick attack.

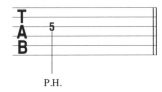

P.H.

HARP HARMONIC: The note is fretted normally and a harmonic is produced by gently resting the pick hand's index finger directly above the indicated fret (in parentheses) while the pick hand's thumb or pick assists by plucking the appropriate string.

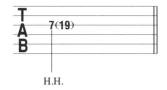

H.H.

PICK SCRAPE: The edge of the pick is rubbed down (or up) the string, producing a scratchy sound.

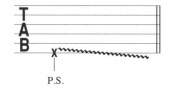

P.S.

MUFFLED STRINGS: A percussive sound is produced by laying the fret hand across the string(s) without depressing, and striking them with the pick hand.

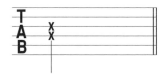

PALM MUTING: The note is partially muted by the pick hand lightly touching the string(s) just before the bridge.

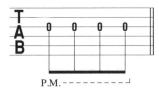

P.M. - - - - - - - - - ⌐

RAKE: Drag the pick across the strings indicated with a single motion.

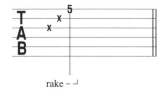

rake - ⌐

TREMOLO PICKING: The note is picked as rapidly and continuously as possible.

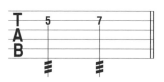

ARPEGGIATE: Play the notes of the chord indicated by quickly rolling them from bottom to top.

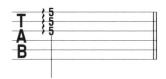

VIBRATO BAR DIVE AND RETURN: The pitch of the note or chord is dropped a specified number of steps (in rhythm), then returned to the original pitch.

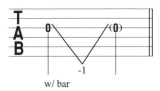

w/ bar

VIBRATO BAR SCOOP: Depress the bar just before striking the note, then quickly release the bar.

w/ bar - - - - - - - ⌐

VIBRATO BAR DIP: Strike the note and then immediately drop a specified number of steps, then release back to the original pitch.

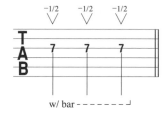

w/ bar - - - - - - - ⌐

Additional Musical Definitions

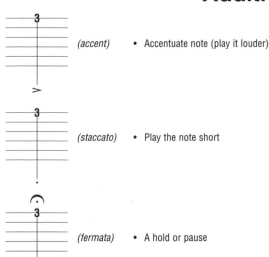

(accent) • Accentuate note (play it louder)

(staccato) • Play the note short

(fermata) • A hold or pause

⊓ • Downstroke

∨ • Upstroke

• Repeat measures between signs

NOTE: Tablature numbers in parentheses are used when:
  • The note is sustained, but a new articulation begins (such as a hammer-on, pull-off, slide, or bend), or
  • A bend is released.
  • A note sustains while crossing from one staff to another.

Hal·Leonard® GUITAR PLAY-ALONG

AUDIO ACCESS INCLUDED

INCLUDES TAB

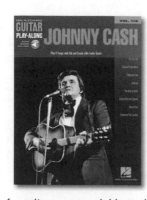

This series will help you play your favorite songs quickly and easily. Just follow the tab and listen to the CD or online audio to hear how the guitar should sound, and then play along using the separate backing tracks. Playback tools are provided for slowing down the tempo without changing pitch and looping challenging parts. The melody and lyrics are included in the book so that you can sing or simply follow along.

89. REGGAE
00700468.................$15.99

90. CLASSICAL POP
00700469.................$14.99

91. BLUES INSTRUMENTALS
00700505.................$17.99

92. EARLY ROCK INSTRUMENTALS
00700506.................$15.99

93. ROCK INSTRUMENTALS
00700507.................$16.99

94. SLOW BLUES
00700508.................$16.99

95. BLUES CLASSICS
00700509.................$15.99

96. BEST COUNTRY HITS
00211615.................$16.99

97. CHRISTMAS CLASSICS
00236542.................$14.99

98. ROCK BAND
00700704.................$14.95

99. ZZ TOP
00700762.................$16.99

100. B.B. KING
00700466.................$16.99

101. SONGS FOR BEGINNERS
00701917.................$14.99

102. CLASSIC PUNK
00700769.................$14.99

103. SWITCHFOOT
00700773.................$16.99

104. DUANE ALLMAN
00700846.................$16.99

105. LATIN
00700939.................$16.99

106. WEEZER
00700958.................$14.99

107. CREAM
00701069.................$16.99

108. THE WHO
00701053.................$16.99

109. STEVE MILLER
00701054.................$17.99

110. SLIDE GUITAR HITS
00701055.................$16.99

111. JOHN MELLENCAMP
00701056.................$14.99

112. QUEEN
00701052.................$16.99

113. JIM CROCE
00701058.................$17.99

114. BON JOVI
00701060.................$16.99

115. JOHNNY CASH
00701070.................$16.99

116. THE VENTURES
00701124.................$16.99

117. BRAD PAISLEY
00701224.................$16.99

118. ERIC JOHNSON
00701353.................$16.99

119. AC/DC CLASSICS
00701356.................$17.99

120. PROGRESSIVE ROCK
00701457.................$14.99

121. U2
00701508.................$16.99

122. CROSBY, STILLS & NASH
00701610.................$16.99

123. LENNON & MCCARTNEY ACOUSTIC
00701614.................$16.99

125. JEFF BECK
00701687.................$16.99

126. BOB MARLEY
00701701.................$16.99

127. 1970S ROCK
00701739.................$16.99

128. 1960S ROCK
00701740.................$14.99

129. MEGADETH
00701741.................$16.99

130. IRON MAIDEN
00701742.................$17.99

131. 1990S ROCK
00701743.................$14.99

132. COUNTRY ROCK
00701757.................$15.99

133. TAYLOR SWIFT
00701894.................$16.99

134. AVENGED SEVENFOLD
00701906.................$16.99

135. MINOR BLUES
00151350.................$17.99

136. GUITAR THEMES
00701922.................$14.99

137. IRISH TUNES
00701966.................$15.99

138. BLUEGRASS CLASSICS
00701967.................$16.99

139. GARY MOORE
00702370.................$16.99

140. MORE STEVIE RAY VAUGHAN
00702396.................$17.99

141. ACOUSTIC HITS
00702401.................$16.99

142. GEORGE HARRISON
00237697.................$17.99

143. SLASH
00702425.................$19.99

144. DJANGO REINHARDT
00702531.................$16.99

145. DEF LEPPARD
00702532.................$17.99

146. ROBERT JOHNSON
00702533.................$16.99

147. SIMON & GARFUNKEL
14041591.................$16.99

148. BOB DYLAN
14041592.................$16.99

149. AC/DC HITS
14041593.................$17.99

150. ZAKK WYLDE
02501717.................$16.99

151. J.S. BACH
02501730.................$16.99

152. JOE BONAMASSA
02501751.................$19.99

153. RED HOT CHILI PEPPERS
00702990.................$19.99

155. ERIC CLAPTON – FROM THE ALBUM UNPLUGGED
00703085.................$16.99

156. SLAYER
00703770.................$17.99

157. FLEETWOOD MAC
00101382.................$16.99

159. WES MONTGOMERY
00102593.................$19.99

160. T-BONE WALKER
00102641.................$17.99

161. THE EAGLES – ACOUSTIC
00102659.................$17.99

162. THE EAGLES HITS
00102667.................$17.99

163. PANTERA
00103036.................$17.99

164. VAN HALEN 1986-1995
00110270.................$17.99

165. GREEN DAY
00210343.................$17.99

166. MODERN BLUES
00700764.................$16.99

167. DREAM THEATER
00111938.................$24.99

168. KISS
00113421.................$16.99

169. TAYLOR SWIFT
00115982.................$16.99

170. THREE DAYS GRACE
00117337.................$16.99

171. JAMES BROWN
00117420.................$16.99

173. TRANS-SIBERIAN ORCHESTRA
00119907.................$19.99

174. SCORPIONS
00122119.................$16.99

175. MICHAEL SCHENKER
00122127.................$16.99

176. BLUES BREAKERS WITH JOHN MAYALL & ERIC CLAPTON
00122132.................$19.99

177. ALBERT KING
00123271.................$16.99

178. JASON MRAZ
00124165.................$17.99

179. RAMONES
00127073.................$16.99

180. BRUNO MARS
00129706.................$16.99

181. JACK JOHNSON
00129854.................$16.99

182. SOUNDGARDEN
00138161.................$17.99

183. BUDDY GUY
00138240.................$17.99

184. KENNY WAYNE SHEPHERD
00138258.................$17.99

185. JOE SATRIANI
00139457.................$17.99

186. GRATEFUL DEAD
00139459.................$17.99

187. JOHN DENVER
00140839.................$17.99

188. MÖTLEY CRUE
00141145.................$17.99

189. JOHN MAYER
00144350.................$17.99

190. DEEP PURPLE
00146152.................$17.99

191. PINK FLOYD CLASSICS
00146164.................$17.99

192. JUDAS PRIEST
00151352.................$17.99

193. STEVE VAI
00156028.................$19.99

195. METALLICA: 1983-1988
00234291.................$19.99

196. METALLICA: 1991-2016
00234292.................$19.99

HAL•LEONARD®

For complete songlists, visit
Hal Leonard online at
www.halleonard.com

Prices, contents, and availability subject to
change without notice.

FIRST 50

The First 50 series steers new players in the right direction. These books contain easy to intermediate arrangements for must-know songs. Each arrangement is simple and streamlined, yet still captures the essence of the tune.

First 50 Blues Songs You Should Play on Guitar

All Your Love (I Miss Loving) • Bad to the Bone • Born Under a Bad Sign • Dust My Broom • Hoodoo Man Blues • I'm Your Hoochie Coochie Man • Killing Floor • Little Red Rooster • Love Struck Baby • Pride and Joy • Smoking Gun • Still Got the Blues • The Thrill Is Gone • Tuff Enuff • You Shook Me • and many more.

00235790 Guitar **$14.99**

First 50 Christmas Carols You Should Play on Guitar

Angels We Have Heard on High • Away in a Manger • Coventry Carol • The First Noel • God Rest Ye Merry, Gentlemen • Good King Wenceslas • The Holly and the Ivy • Jingle Bells • O Christmas Tree • O Come, All Ye Faithful • Silent Night • The Twelve Days of Christmas • Up on the Housetop • We Wish You a Merry Christmas • What Child Is This? • and more.

00236224 Guitar **$12.99**

First 50 Christmas Songs You Should Play on Guitar

All I Want for Christmas Is My Two Front Teeth • Blue Christmas • The Christmas Song (Chestnuts Roasting on an Open Fire) • Do You Want to Build a Snowman? • Feliz Navidad • Happy Xmas (War Is Over) • I'll Be Home for Christmas • Mary, Did You Know? • Rudolph the Red-Nosed Reindeer • Santa Baby • Silent Night • White Christmas • Winter Wonderland • and more.

00147009 Guitar **$14.99**

First 50 Classical Pieces You Should Play on Guitar

This collection includes compositions by J.S. Bach, Augustin Barrios, Matteo Carcassi, Domenico Scarlatti, Fernando Sor, Francisco Tárrega, Robert de Visée, Antonio Vivaldi and many more.

00155414 Solo Guitar **$14.99**

First 50 Folk Songs You Should Play on Guitar

Amazing Grace • Down by the Riverside • Home on the Range • I've Been Working on the Railroad • Kumbaya • Man of Constant Sorrow • Nobody Knows the Trouble I've Seen • Oh! Susanna • She'll Be Comin' 'Round the Mountain • This Little Light of Mine • When the Saints Go Marching In • The Yellow Rose of Texas • and more.

00235868 Guitar **$14.99**

First 50 Jazz Standards You Should Play on Guitar

All the Things You Are • Body and Soul • Don't Get Around Much Anymore • Fly Me to the Moon (In Other Words) • The Girl from Ipanema (Garota De Ipanema) • I Got Rhythm • Laura • Misty • Night and Day • Satin Doll • Summertime • When I Fall in Love • and more.

00198594 Solo Guitar **$14.99**

First 50 Rock Songs You Should Play on Electric Guitar

All Along the Watchtower • Beat It • Born to Be Wild • Brown Eyed Girl • Cocaine • Detroit Rock City • Hallelujah • (I Can't Get No) Satisfaction • Iron Man • Oh, Pretty Woman • Pride and Joy • Seven Nation Army • Should I Stay or Should I Go • Smells like Teen Spirit • Smoke on the Water • When I Come Around • Wild Thing • You Really Got Me • and more.

00131159 Guitar **$14.99**

First 50 Songs You Should Fingerpick on Guitar

Annie's Song • Blackbird • The Boxer • Classical Gas • Dust in the Wind • Fire and Rain • Greensleeves • Hell Hound on My Trail • Is There Anybody Out There? • Julia • Puff the Magic Dragon • Road Trippin' • Shape of My Heart • Tears in Heaven • Time in a Bottle • Vincent (Starry Starry Night) • The Wind • and more.

00149269 Solo Guitar **$14.99**

First 50 Songs You Should Play on Acoustic Guitar

Against the Wind • Barely Breathing • Boulevard of Broken Dreams • Champagne Supernova • Crazy Little Thing Called Love • Every Rose Has Its Thorn • Fast Car • Free Fallin' • Ho Hey • I Won't Give Up • Layla • Let Her Go • Mean • One • Ring of Fire • Signs • Stairway to Heaven • Trouble • Wagon Wheel • Wish You Were Here • Yellow • Yesterday • and more.

00131209 Guitar **$14.99**

First 50 Songs You Should Strum on Guitar

American Pie • Blowin' in the Wind • Daughter • Good Riddance (Time of Your Life) • Hey, Soul Sister • Home • I Will Wait • Losing My Religion • Mrs. Robinson • No Woman No Cry • Peaceful Easy Feeling • Rocky Mountain High • Sweet Caroline • Teardrops on My Guitar • Wonderful Tonight • You're Still the One • and more.

00148996 Guitar **$14.99**

Prices, content and availability subject to change without notice.

www.halleonard.com